Oracle SQL*Plus
Pocket Reference

THIRD EDITION

Oracle SQL*Plus
Pocket Reference

Jonathan Gennick

Beijing · Cambridge · Farnham · Köln · Paris · Sebastopol · Taipei · Tokyo

Oracle SQL*Plus Pocket Reference, Third Edition

by Jonathan Gennick

Published by O'Reilly Media, Inc., 1005 Gravenstein Highway North,
Sebastopol, CA 95472.

O'Reilly books may be purchased for educational, business, or sales
promotional use. Online editions are also available for most titles
(*safari.oreilly.com*). For more information, contact our corporate/
institutional sales department: (800) 998-9938 or *corporate@oreilly.com*.

Editor:	Deborah Russell
Production Editor:	Claire Cloutier
Cover Designer:	Ellie Volckhausen
Interior Designer:	David Futato

Printing History:

April 2000:	First Edition.
October 2002:	Second Edition.
November 2004:	Third Edition.

0-596-00885-6
[C]

Contents

Oracle SQL*Plus Pocket Reference

Introduction

The *Oracle SQL*Plus Pocket Reference* is a quick reference guide to SQL*Plus and to frequently used SQL statements. The purpose of this book is to help you find the syntax of specific language elements, including those in Oracle Database 10*g*. It is not a self-contained user guide; basic knowledge of SQL*Plus and SQL is assumed. For more detail and for tutorial information about SQL and SQL*Plus, see my book *Oracle SQL*Plus: The Definitive Guide* (O'Reilly). *Mastering Oracle SQL* by Sanjay Mishra and Alan Beaulieu (O'Reilly) is a good resource if you need advanced help with SQL. My own *SQL Pocket Guide* (O'Reilly) is, I hope, a good resource for those working with SQL on multiple platforms.

SQL sections within this book include the following:

> Selecting Data
> Modeling Data
> Inserting Data
> Updating Data
> Deleting Data
> Merging Data (Oracle9*i* and Higher)
> Transaction Management

The rest of the book is devoted to SQL*Plus.

Acknowledgments

Deborah Russell, Darl Kuhn, Ken Jacobs, John Haydu, and Alison Holloway all played a part in making this book a reality. For their assistance and support, I'm most grateful.

Conventions

UPPERCASE
> Indicates SQL*Plus, SQL, or PL/SQL keywords

lowercase
> Indicates user-defined items such as table names

Italic
> Indicates filenames, URLs, usernames, passwords, emphasis, and introduction of new terms

`Constant width`
> Used for code examples

`Constant width italic`
> Indicates an element of syntax you need to supply in a SQL*Plus command or SQL statement

`Constant width bold`
> Indicates user input in examples showing an interaction; also used for emphasis in code examples

[ ]
> Used in syntax descriptions to denote optional elements

{ }
> Used in syntax descriptions to denote a required choice

|
> Used in syntax descriptions to separate choices and optional elements

_
> Used in syntax descriptions to indicate that the underlined option is the default

Command-Line SQL*Plus

This section covers information essential for interacting with command-line SQL*Plus. Here, you will learn how to start SQL*Plus, enter commands, delimit strings, and name variables.

Starting SQL*Plus

Invoke SQL*Plus by issuing the *sqlplus* command from your operating system command prompt. On Microsoft Windows systems, use either *sqlplus* or *sqlplusw*, depending on whether you want SQL*Plus to run in a command-prompt window or in its own window; you can also select an icon from the Start menu. (Early releases of SQL*Plus on Windows used executable names such as *PLUS33* and *PLUS80W.*)

WARNING

Beware of passing your password as a command-line argument to SQL*Plus. Such passwords may be easily visible to other users on Linux and Unix systems.

Syntax for the sqlplus command

The syntax used to invoke SQL*Plus is as follows:

```
sqlplus [options] [logon] [start]

options ::= option [option...]

option ::= {-H[ELP]
           |-V[ERSION]
           |-C[OMPATIBILITY] x.y[.z]
           |-L[OGON]
           |-M[ARKUP] markup
           |-R[ESTRICT] {1 | 2 | 3}
           |-S[ILENT]}
```

```
markup ::= HTML [ON | OFF]
             [HEAD text] [BODY text] [TABLE text]
             [ENTMAP {ON | OFF}] [PREFORMAT {ON | OFF}]

logon ::= {typical | os_authenticated
           |administrative | /NOLOG}

typical ::= username[/password][@net_service_name]

os_authenticated ::= /

administrative ::= {typical | os_authenticated}
                   AS {SYSDBA | SYSOPER}

start ::= @{url | file_path} [param [param...]]
```

The -RESTRICT and -MARKUP parameters were introduced in
Oracle8i Database. -HELP and -VERSION were introduced in
Oracle9i Database. Here are the parameter descriptions:

-H[ELP]

Displays the syntax for the *sqlplus* command and then
exits.

-V[ERSION]

Displays the current SQL*Plus version number and related
information, then exits.

-C[OMPATIBILITY]*x.y*[*.z*]

Specifies a prior version (*x*), a release (*y*), and optionally, an
update (*z*) of SQL*Plus with which you wish to be compatible.

-L[OGON]

Inhibits reprompting for a username and password should
the initial login credentials prove invalid. Use this option
when invoking SQL*Plus from, say, a *cron* job, where
reprompting makes no sense, because there is no interac-
tive user to see and respond to the prompt.

-M[ARKUP] *markup*

Controls whether SQL*Plus output is in plain text or
HTML. If in HTML, further specifies various options.

-R[ESTRICT] {1 | 2 | 3}

Disables commands that interact with the operating system. You may choose from one of three restriction levels:

1 Disables EDIT and HOST commands

2 Disables EDIT, HOST, SAVE, SPOOL, and STORE

3 Disables EDIT, GET, HOST, SAVE, SPOOL, START, @, @@, and STORE

In addition, level 3 prevents the execution of the user profile script in *login.sql*.

-S[ILENT]

Tells SQL*Plus to run in silent mode. No startup messages, such as the copyright message, will be displayed. No command prompt will be displayed, and no commands will be echoed to the screen. This option is useful if you are invoking SQL*Plus from within some other program and want to do it transparently. Normally, you would use this option in conjunction with invoking a script file.

HTML [ON | OFF]

Enables or disables HTML output. The default is HTML OFF.   *sql plus -m "HTML ON"*

[HEAD *text*]

Specifies content for the HEAD tag, which ends up as <HEAD>*text*</HEAD>.

[BODY *text*]

Specifies attributes for the BODY tag, which ends up as <BODY *text*>.

[TABLE *text*]

Specifies attributes for the TABLE tag used to define tables holding query output, which ends up as <TABLE *text*>. Tables used to hold page headers and footers are not affected by this parameter.

[ENTMAP {ON | OFF}]

Specifies whether SQL*Plus replaces special characters
such as "<" and ">" with their corresponding HTML
entities (e.g., "<" and ">"). The default is ENT-
MAP ON.

[PREFORMAT {ON | OFF}]

Matters only when HTML output is enabled, and specifies
whether SQL*Plus writes query output as an HTML table
or as a preformatted text block (using <pre>...</pre>).
The default is PREFORMAT OFF.

/NOLOG

Starts SQL*Plus without a database connection.

typical ::= *username*[/*password*][@*net_service_name*]

Authenticates you using the given username, password,
and net service name. Net service names are often, but
not always, defined in a file known as *tnsnames.ora*.

administrative ::= { *typical* | *os_authenticated*}
    AS {SYSDBA | SYSOPER}

Authenticates you as either a database administrator
(SYSDBA) or operator (SYSOPER).

@{*url* | *file_path*}

Invokes a SQL*Plus script via either a URL or a path and
filename. URLs may be either *http://* or *ftp://*. Filenames
may include paths and extensions. The default file extension is *.sql*.

[*param* [*param*...]]

Specify one or more parameters to pass to a script that
you are invoking.

Entering Commands

How you enter commands in SQL*Plus depends on whether
you are entering a command to SQL*Plus itself, or are entering a SQL statement or a PL/SQL block.

Entering SQL*Plus commands

Commands such as COLUMN, DESCRIBE, SET, and TTI-TLE (and all the others listed later in the "SQL*Plus Command Reference") are commands to SQL*Plus itself. These commands must be entered on one line and are executed immediately after you enter them. For example:

```
SET ECHO ON
DESCRIBE employee
```

SQL*Plus commands may optionally be terminated by a semicolon. For example:

```
PROMPT This semicolon won't print.;
CONNECT system/manager;
```

You can change the way SQL*Plus behaves toward semicolons by changing the SQLTERMINATOR setting.

Long SQL*Plus commands may be continued onto multiple physical lines. The SQL*Plus continuation character is a hyphen (-). Use it at the end of a physical line to continue a long SQL*Plus command to the next line. The following three lines, for example, are treated as one by SQL*Plus:

```
COLUMN employee_id -
FORMAT 099999 -
HEADING 'Emp ID'
```

The space in front of the continuation character is optional. Quoted strings may also be continued. For example:

```
SELECT 'Hello-
World!' FROM dual;
```

When you continue a quoted string, any spaces before the continuation character are included in the string. The line break also counts as one space.

Entering SQL statements

SQL statements may span multiple lines and must always be terminated. This may be done using either a semicolon (;) or a forward slash (/).

For example:

```
SELECT user
FROM dual;

SELECT user
FROM dual
/
```

In both cases, the SQL statement is entered into a buffer
known as the *SQL buffer* and is executed. You may also terminate a SQL statement using either a blank line or a period,
in which case the statement is stored in the buffer but not
executed. For example:

```
SQL> SELECT user
  2  FROM dual
  3
SQL> SELECT user
  2  FROM dual
  3  .
```

Use the SET SQLTERMINATOR command to change the
terminator from a semicolon to some other character. Use
SET SQLBLANKLINES ON to allow blank lines within a
SQL statement. To execute the statement currently in the
buffer, enter a forward slash on a line by itself.

Entering PL/SQL blocks

PL/SQL blocks may span multiple lines and may contain
blank lines. They must be terminated by either a forward
slash or a period (.) on a line by itself. For example:

```
BEGIN
   DBMS_OUTPUT.PUT_LINE('Hello World!');
END;
/

BEGIN
   DBMS_OUTPUT.PUT_LINE('Hello World!');
END;
.
```

When a forward slash is used, the block is sent to the server and executed immediately. When a period is used, the block is stored only in the SQL buffer. Use the SET BLOCKTERMINATOR command to change the block terminator from a period to some other character.

Strings in SQL*Plus Commands

Many SQL*Plus-specific commands take string values as parameters. Simple strings containing no spaces or punctuation characters may be entered without quotes. Here's an example:

```
COLUMN employee_id HEADING emp_id
```

Generally, it's safer to use quoted strings. Either single or double quotes may be used. For example:

```
COLUMN employee_id HEADING 'Emp #'
COLUMN employee_id HEADING "Emp #"
```

To embed quotes in a string, either double them or use a different enclosing quote. The following two commands have equivalent results:

```
COLUMN employee_id HEADING '''Emp #'''
COLUMN employee_id HEADING "'Emp #'"
```

The single exception to these rules is the PROMPT command. All quotes used in a PROMPT command will appear in the output.

Specifying Filenames

Several SQL*Plus commands allow you to specify a filename. In all cases, you may also include a path and/or an extension with the name. For example:

```
SPOOL my_report
SPOOL c:\temp\my_report
SPOOL create_synonyms.sql
```

Most file-related commands assume a default extension if you don't supply one. The default varies by command.

& var-name - 1st usage

&& var-name - subsequent us[e]
without prompt[?]

Naming Variables

SQL*Plus allows you to declare two types of variables: *user variables* and *bind variables*. The rules for naming each type are different.

User variable names may contain letters, digits, and underscores (_) in any order. They are case-insensitive and are limited to 30 characters in length.

Bind variable names must begin with a letter, but then may contain letters, digits, underscores, dollar signs ($), and number signs (#). They are also case-insensitive and limited to 30 characters in length.

Browser-Based SQL*Plus

In 2001, Oracle released *i*SQL*Plus, a browser-based version of SQL*Plus that runs in a three-tier configuration. You access *i*SQL*Plus via a web browser on your PC. Beginning in Oracle Database 10*g*, *i*SQL*Plus runs as a Java 2 Enterprise Edition (J2EE) application server. It is installed by default with the database and runs on the database server.

*i*SQL*Plus is as compatible as possible with command-line SQL*Plus, but there are a few differences. Most obviously, the editing paradigm is different. You enter and edit commands using a text box in your browser window. Line-editing commands such as CHANGE and APPEND make no sense in that context and are not supported in *i*SQL*Plus. The "SQL*Plus Command Reference" section indicates which commands do not apply in *i*SQL*Plus.

Another difference between *i*SQL*Plus and command-line SQL*Plus involves access to operating system files. Commands such as GET and SPOOL are disabled in *i*SQL*Plus. The general rule is that you are not allowed any kind of access to operating system files.

Starting and Stopping iSQL*Plus

Before you can use *i*SQL*Plus, you need to start the application server. Do that first by connecting to your database server as the Oracle software owner and then by entering the *isqlplusctl start* command:

```
oracle@gennick02:~> isqlplusctl start
iSQL*Plus 10.1.0.2.0
Copyright (c) 2004 Oracle.  All rights reserved.
Starting iSQL*Plus ...
iSQL*Plus started.
```

Clients may now connect to *i*SQL*Plus via their browsers.

Use *isqlplusctl stop* to shut down the *i*SQL*Plus application server.

Connecting to iSQL*Plus

Start *i*SQL*Plus in your web browser by entering a URL. In Oracle Database 10*g*, the default URL takes the following form:

```
http://server.domain.com:5560/isqlplus
```

Thus, to connect to *i*SQL*Plus running on the database server named *gennick01.gennick.com*, you would enter the following URL:

```
http://gennick01.gennick.com:5560/isqlplus
```

5560 is the default port number used by *i*SQL*Plus since Oracle9*i* Database Release 2. In Oracle9*i* Database Release 1, the default *i*SQL*Plus port was 80.

Your database administrator (DBA) may have changed the port number. If you have doubts about the URL, ask your DBA. If you *are* the DBA, you can determine the currently used port number by looking in one of the following files:

Oracle9*i* Database (Unix/Linux)
    $ORACLE_HOME/Apache/bin/conf/httpd.conf

Oracle9*i* Database (Windows)
    %ORACLE_HOME%\Apache\Apache\conf\httpd.conf

Oracle Database 10g
    *$ORACLE_HOME/oc4j/j2ee/isqlplus/config/http-web-site.
    xml*

When you successfully connect to the *i*SQL*Plus application server, you'll be taken to the *i*SQL*Plus login page shown in Figure 1, which asks for your username, your password, and a connect identifier.

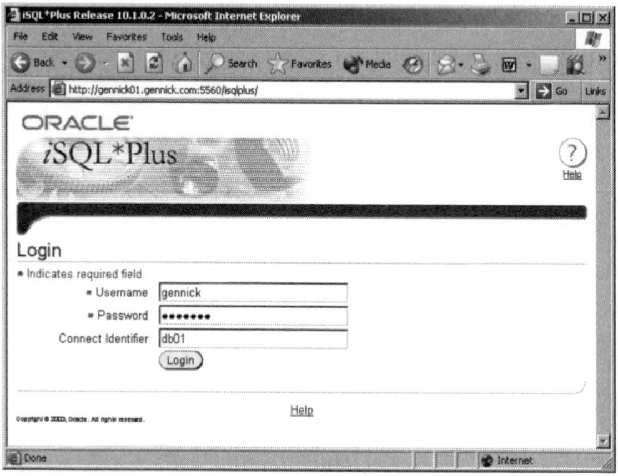

*Figure 1. The iSQL*Plus login page*

Connecting to a Database

To connect to a database, enter your login information as shown in Figure 1. Be aware that any *connect identifier* (or a *net service name*) that you enter is resolved on the server that is running *i*SQL*Plus. Thus, entries in your own *tnsnames. ora* file have no effect. What matters are the entries in *tnsnames.ora* on the machine serving *i*SQL*Plus. Leave the connect identifier blank to connect to the default database on the remote machine.

Once you've connected and have a workspace (Figure 2), you can connect to other databases by issuing the same kind of CONNECT command that you might issue from command-line SQL*Plus. Again, any net service name that you specify is resolved on the *i*SQL*Plus application server.

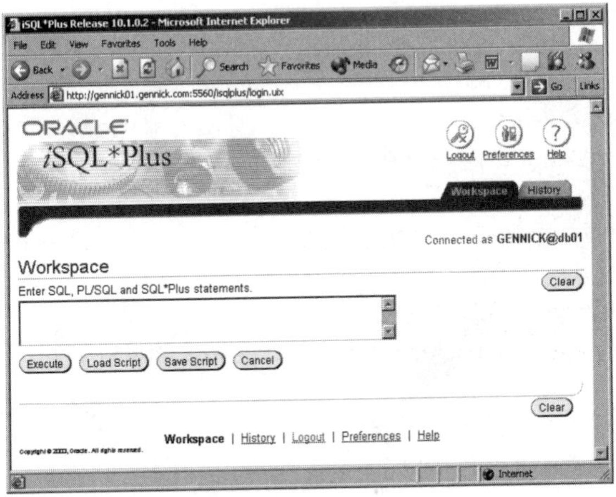

*Figure 2. The iSQL*Plus workspace*

Connecting as SYSDBA

In Oracle Database 10*g*, you can use a special URL to connect to *i*SQL*Plus in either the SYSDBA or SYSOPER administrative roles. By default, this URL is */dba* appended onto the end of the standard URL. For example:

```
http://gennick02.gennick.com:5560/isqlplus/dba
```

When you connect to *i*SQL*Plus as a DBA, you must authenticate twice, as in the following process:

1. Enter a special URL that brings up the *i*SQL*Plus DBA login dialog (Figure 3).

2. Enter a username and password to identify yourself to *i*SQL*Plus as a DBA. This username/password has meaning only to *i*SQL*Plus and is unrelated to your database username/password. For more about this, see the next section, "Creating SYSDBA Users."

3. *i*SQL*Plus takes you to a special version of the login page that includes a pulldown menu for choosing between SYSDBA and SYSOPER.

4. Authenticate to your database using your database username and password.

You can then proceed to use *i*SQL*Plus for administrative tasks such as starting and stopping your database instance.

Figure 3. The iSQL*Plus DBA login dialog

Creating SYSDBA Users

To authenticate you as a DBA, *i*SQL*Plus uses a Java Authentication and Authorization Service (JAAS) provider named Java AuthoriZatioN, which Oracle simply refers to as JAZN. You must create a username and password within JAZN in order to use *i*SQL*Plus as SYSDBA or SYSOPER. Follow these steps:

1. Log into your database server as the Oracle software owner, or as a user having the DBA role.

2. Create a JAVA_HOME environment variable:

   ```
   export JAVA_HOME=$ORACLE_HOME/jdk
   ```

3. It is extremely critical to invoke the JAZN utility from the correct directory. If you fail to do so, the authentication process will also fail. Set your current working directory as follows:

   ```
   cd $ORACLE_HOME/oc4j/j2ee/isqlplus
       /application-deployments/isqlplus
   ```

4. Invoke the JAZN shell for the "*i*SQL*Plus DBA" realm, as the *admin* user, using the following (rather horrendous) command. Type it as one long line. Type it exactly as shown, including the hyphens (-), but supply your own password if you've changed it from the default of *welcome*:

   ```
   $JAVA_HOME/bin/java -Djava.security.properties=
   $ORACLE_HOME/sqlplus/admin/iplus/provider -jar
   $ORACLE_HOME/oc4j/j2ee/home/jazn.jar -user
   "iSQL*Plus DBA/admin" -password welcome -shell
   ```

5. Issue an *adduser* command to create a new *i*SQL*Plus DBA user. The following example creates a user named *dude* with a password of *secret*:

   ```
   JAZN:> adduser "iSQL*Plus DBA" dude secret
   ```

6. Grant the *webDba* role to the user you just created:

   ```
   JAZN:> grantrole webDba "iSQL*Plus DBA" dude
   ```

7. If this is your first time using the JAZN shell, change the *admin* password to something other than the default. The following example changes the *admin* password from *welcome* to *secret*:

```
JAZN:> setpasswd "iSQL*Plus DBA"
         admin welcome secret
```

8. Exit the JAZN utility:

```
JAZN:> exit
```

In order for *i*SQL*Plus to see the new JAZN user you have created, you'll need to bounce *i*SQL*Plus by issuing the command *isqlplusctl stop* followed by *isqlplusctl start*.

Entering and Executing Commands

From the Workspace page, enter and execute commands by typing them into the large text box and then pressing the Execute button below the text box. Query results are shown in the form of an HTML table. There may be a Next Page button below the table for you to use in cycling through multiple pages of output.

You may enter and execute one command (or statement or block) at a time, or you may execute multiple commands in succession. To execute multiple commands in succession, simply type them into the text box as you would into a script file.

Getting Output as Plain Text

Use the following command to get plain text output rather than an HTML table, which is handy if you wish to copy and paste results into some other application:

```
SET MARKUP HTML PREFORMAT ON
```

For those who are strongly GUI-oriented, *i*SQL*Plus provides a Script Formatting preferences page from which you

---

can toggle the PREFORMAT setting using a radio button. Follow these steps:

1. Click on the Preferences button next to the Logout button.

2. Look on the left side of the resulting page under the heading System Configuration, click on Script Formatting, then scroll way down to the Preformatted Output radio buttons.

3. Choose whichever option you prefer, scroll to the bottom of the page, and click the Apply button.

4. Click the Workspace tab to return to the Workspace page.

Executing Scripts

To execute a script from your local hard drive, follow these steps:

1. Click the Load Script button. You'll see the page shown in Figure 4.

Figure 4. Loading a script from your workstation's hard drive

2. Click the Browse button to open a file chooser dialog.

3. Navigate to the file you want, select it, and click the OK button. You'll be brought back to the page shown in Figure 4 and the File text box will be filled in with the path to the file you chose.

4. Click either Load button. The file will be loaded and placed into the text box in the Workspace page.

5. Optionally edit the script you are about to execute.

6. Click the Execute button to run the script.

The Load Script functionality is also helpful if you want to look at the contents of a SQL script that you would otherwise execute from a web server using the @ command. You can type the script's URL into the URL text box (in place of Step 3) and click the Load button; iSQL*Plus will load the script into the Workspace text box for you to look at, edit, and possibly execute.

You can execute scripts using the START, @, and @@ commands, but only via *http* or *ftp*. For example, you can issue the command @*http://gennick.com/message* to execute a script from the Internet, but you *cannot* issue @*message* to execute a *message.sql* file on the application server.

Disconnecting from iSQL*Plus

There are two ways to end an iSQL*Plus session. You can click the Logout button in the upper right of the page, or you can issue the SQL*Plus DISCONNECT command.

It's best to log out or disconnect when you're done using SQL*Plus. However, there is a timeout, so if you just close your browser, or even if you walk away for coffee, the iSQL*Plus application server will eventually terminate your session.

Selecting Data

The SELECT statement is the key to getting data out of an Oracle database. It's also very likely the most commonly executed SQL statement from SQL*Plus.

The SELECT Statement

The basic form of the SELECT statement looks like this:

```
WITH subqueries
SELECT column_list
FROM table_list
WHERE conditions
GROUP BY column_list
HAVING conditions
ORDER BY column_list;
```

The lists in this syntax are comma-delimited. The column list, for example, is a comma-delimited list of column names or expressions identifying the data you want the query to return.

Selecting columns from a table

To retrieve columns from a table, list the columns you want after the SELECT keyword, place the table name after the FROM keyword, and execute your statement. The following query returns a list of tables you own with the names of their assigned tablespaces:

```
SELECT table_name, tablespace_name
FROM user_tables;
```

Ordering query results

You can use the ORDER BY clause to sort the results of a query. The following example sorts the results by table name:

```
SELECT table_name, tablespace_name
FROM user_tables
ORDER BY table_name;
```

The default is to sort in ascending order. You can specify descending order using the DESC keyword. For example:

```
ORDER BY table_name DESC;
```

While it's redundant, ASC may be used to specify ascending order. The following example sorts the table list first by tablespace name in descending order, and then within that by table name in ascending order:

```
SELECT table_name, tablespace_name
FROM user_tables
ORDER BY tablespace_name DESC,
         table_name ASC;
```

If you want the sort to be case-insensitive, you can use Oracle's built-in UPPER function. For example:

```
SELECT table_name, tablespace_name
FROM user_tables
ORDER BY UPPER(table_name);
```

For symmetry, Oracle also has a built-in LOWER function. LOWER converts a string to lowercase; UPPER converts to uppercase.

Restricting query results

Use the WHERE clause to restrict the rows returned by a query to those that you need to see. The following example returns a list of any invalid objects that you own:

```
SELECT object_name, object_type
FROM user_objects
WHERE status = 'INVALID'
ORDER BY object_type, object_name;
```

The expression following the WHERE clause may be any valid Boolean expression. Oracle supports all the typical operators you'd expect: +, -, /, *, <, >, <>, <=, >=, AND, OR, NOT, ||, IS NULL, LIKE, BETWEEN, and IN. Parentheses are also supported and may be used to clarify and specify the order of evaluation.

rownum

Using column aliases

If a SELECT statement includes columns that are expressions, Oracle generates a column name based on the expression. Take a look at the following SQL statement:

```
SELECT SUM(hours_logged)
FROM project_hours
WHERE project_id = 1001;
```

The name of the column returned by this query will be SUM(HOURS_LOGGED). That means that any COLUMN commands used to format the output need to look like this:

```
COLUMN SUM(HOURS_LOGGED) HEADING 'Total Hours'
```

As your expressions become more complicated, the Oracle-generated names become difficult to deal with. It's better to use a column alias to supply a more user-friendly name for the computed column. For example:

```
SELECT SUM(hours_logged) total_hours
FROM project_hours
WHERE project_id = 1001;
```

Now the column name is obvious. It's TOTAL_HOURS, and it won't change even if the expression changes.

Factoring out subqueries

You can use the WITH clause to create named result sets from subqueries. You can then select from these result sets many times in the main query. For example, the following query returns a list of employees whose billing rates are in the top half of the range:

```
SELECT employee_id id, employee_billing_rate rate,
       (SELECT MAX(employee_billing_rate)
        FROM employee) top_rate
FROM employee
WHERE employee_billing_rate >
      (SELECT MAX(employee_billing_rate)
       FROM employee) / 2;
```

The results are as follows:

```
        ID       RATE   TOP_RATE
---------- ---------- ----------
       101        169        300
       108        220        300
       113        300        300
```

Using the WITH clause, you can factor the subquery's
SELECT MAX logic out of the main query and into a named
subquery. In the following version of the query, the SELECT
MAX logic to compute the maximum billing rate appears
only one time:

```
WITH top_rate AS
    (SELECT MAX(employee_billing_rate) as rate
     FROM employee)
SELECT employee_id id, employee_billing_rate rate,
    (SELECT rate FROM top_rate)
FROM employee
WHERE employee_billing_rate >
    (SELECT rate FROM top_rate) / 2;
```

You still do need to SELECT values from the named result
sets (top_rate in this case). In this example, the SELECT
MAX subquery is so simple that the WITH version of the
query almost appears more, not less, complex than the non-
WITH version. However, as subqueries get more complex,
the benefits of using WITH (in terms of making queries sim-
pler and more understandable) become more apparent.

You can name multiple result sets in the WITH clause. Simply separate their definitions by commas. The following
example creates a result set named top_rate with the maximum billing rate, followed by a second result set named
rate_threshold. Note the comma following the definition of
top_rate:

```
WITH top_rate AS
    (SELECT MAX(employee_billing_rate) as rate
     FROM employee),
     rate_threshold AS
    (SELECT MAX(employee_billing_rate) / 2 as rate
     FROM employee)
```

```
SELECT employee_id id, employee_billing_rate rate,
       (SELECT rate FROM top_rate)
FROM employee
WHERE employee_billing_rate >
       (SELECT rate FROM rate_threshold);
```

In some, but not all, cases you will see a performance benefit from using WITH to factor out subqueries that otherwise might execute multiple times. In this section's example, on my test database, the WITH version of the query was notably less efficient: it consistently required 8 "db block gets", 23 "consistent gets" and 1 "physical read" as compared to 0, 22, and 0 respectively for the non-WITH version. I have seen other cases in which using WITH had a significant, positive impact on performance. Don't assume anything. Test your queries both ways, to see which performs best.

Nulls

Nulls are pernicious, especially in the WHERE clause of a query. With only a few exceptions, any expression containing a null returns a null as the result. Because nulls are considered neither true nor false, this can have unexpected ramifications on how a WHERE clause is evaluated. Consider the following query that attempts to retrieve a list of NUMBER columns with a scale other than 2:

```
SELECT table_name, column_name
FROM user_tab_columns
WHERE data_type = 'NUMBER'
AND data_scale <> 2;
```

This query is an utter failure because it misses all the floating-point NUMBER columns that have no scale defined at all. Avoid this problem by explicitly considering nulls when you write your WHERE clause. Use either the IS NULL or the IS NOT NULL operator. For example:

```
SELECT table_name, column_name
FROM user_tab_columns
WHERE data_type = 'NUMBER'
AND (data_scale <> 2
OR data_scale IS NULL);
```

When sorting data, nulls are treated as greater than all other values. When a standard ascending sort is done, nulls sort to the bottom of the list. A descending sort causes nulls to rise to the top. You can use the built-in NVL or COALESCE (Oracle9i Database) functions to modify this behavior.

Using the NVL function

If you wish to return results from a query that might be null or to sort results that might be null, you can use Oracle's built-in NVL function to replace nulls with a selected value. For example, the NUM_ROWS column in the USER_TABLES view has a value only for tables that have been analyzed. Here, the NVL function converts nulls to zeros:

```
SELECT table_name, NVL(num_rows,0)
FROM user_tables
ORDER BY NVL(num_rows,0);
```

Be cautious about using NVL in a WHERE clause. Using NVL, or any other function, on an indexed column in a WHERE clause may prevent Oracle from using any index on that column.

Using the COALESCE function

New in Oracle9i Database, the COALESCE function extends the concept behind NVL. You can pass in any number of values as parameters, and COALESCE returns the first non-null value as its result. Consider this nested NVL invocation:

```
SELECT NVL(employee_nickname,
           NVL(employee_first_name,
               employee_last_name))
FROM employee;
```

The nesting of the calls to NVL makes it difficult to decipher the goal of this query. In Oracle9i Database and higher, you can write the query much more simply using the COALESCE function:

```
SELECT COALESCE(employee_nickname,
                employee_first_name,
                employee_last_name)
FROM employee;
```

This query returns each employee's nickname. If there is no nickname for an employee, then the first name is returned instead. If there is no first name, the last name is returned. COALESCE makes this order of preference much more obvious than in the previous NVL solution.

If all parameters to COALESCE are null, the function returns a null result. You can avoid a null result by making your final parameter a constant rather than a column name.

CASE Expressions

CASE expressions represent an ANSI-standard mechanism for embedding IF...THEN...ELSE logic in a SQL statement. Prior to the introduction of CASE, you had to use the Oracle-specific DECODE function to implement conditional logic in a SQL statement. CASE expressions may be used in SELECT lists, WHERE clauses, HAVING clauses, and anywhere else an expression is valid.

TIP

CASE was introduced in Oracle8i, but was enhanced in Oracle9i Database by the addition of searched CASE expressions. In Oracle8i Database, CASE did not work from SQL statements written into PL/SQL blocks.

Simple CASE expressions

Simple CASE expressions are closest in concept to the DECODE function. Their general form is:

```
CASE expression
WHEN expression_1 THEN return_expression_1
WHEN expression_2 THEN return_expression_2
...
ELSE return_expression
END
```

The ELSE portion of the CASE expression is optional. The following is an example of a simple CASE expression:

```
SELECT course_name,
       CASE period
           WHEN 1 THEN 'First'
           WHEN 2 THEN 'Second'
           WHEN 3 THEN 'Third'
           WHEN 4 THEN 'Fourth'
           WHEN 5 THEN 'Fifth'
           ELSE 'Unknown'
           END period_name
FROM course;
```

The period_name following the END keyword is a column alias. It's not necessary, but when using SQL*Plus, it's sometimes helpful to name columns that are the result of an expression.

The equivalent DECODE expression is as follows:

```
SELECT course_name,
       DECODE(period,1,'First',2,'Second',3,'Third',
                     4,'Fourth',5,'Fifth',
                     'Unknown') period_name
FROM course;
```

CASE is part of the SQL standard, whereas DECODE is not. Thus, the use of CASE is preferable when you have a choice.

Searched CASE expressions

A searched CASE expression allows you to do more than match on a single value. A searched CASE allows you to match on expressions:

```
SELECT course_name,
       CASE WHEN period >= 1
            AND period <= 3 THEN 'Morning'
            WHEN period >= 4
            AND period <= 6 THEN 'Afternoon'
            ELSE 'After School'
            END
FROM course;
```

Searched CASE expressions are versatile and enable you to do things easily that were previously difficult or impossible.

Table Joins (Oracle8i and Earlier)

It's very common to combine data from two or more tables to return related information. Such a combination is referred to as a *join*.

Join two tables by listing them in the FROM clause, separated by commas. For example:

```
SELECT user_constraints.constraint_name,
       user_constraints.constraint_type,
       user_cons_columns.column_name
FROM user_constraints, user_cons_columns;
```

This query returns the *Cartesian product*—all possible combinations of all rows from both tables. Conceptually, this is where all joins start. In practice, you almost always put some conditions in the WHERE clause so that only related rows are combined. The following, more useful, query returns a list of constraint names together with the columns involved in each constraint:

```
SELECT user_constraints.constraint_name,
       user_constraints.constraint_type,
       user_cons_columns.column_name
FROM user_constraints, user_cons_columns
WHERE user_constraints.constraint_name
    = user_cons_columns.constraint_name;
```

Because both tables contain columns with matching names, the column references must be qualified with the table name. You can see that this quickly gets cumbersome. The solution is to provide a shorter alias for each table and use that alias to qualify the column names. For example:

```
SELECT uc.constraint_name,
       uc.constraint_type,
       ucc.column_name
FROM user_constraints uc,
     user_cons_columns ucc
WHERE uc.constraint_name =
    ucc.constraint_name;
```

Here, the alias uc is used for the USER_CONSTRAINTS table, while ucc is used for USER_CONS_COLUMNS. The resulting query is much easier to read because you aren't overwhelmed with long table names.

Inner and outer joins

The joins that you have seen so far are inner joins. An *inner join* returns data only when both tables have a row that matches the join conditions. For example, the following query returns only tables that have constraints defined on them:

```
SELECT ut.table_name, uc.constraint_name
FROM user_tables ut, user_constraints uc
WHERE ut.table_name = uc.table_name;
```

An *outer join* returns rows for one table, even when there are no matching rows in the other. Specify an outer join in Oracle by placing a plus sign (+) in parentheses following the column names from the optional table in your WHERE clause. For example:

```
SELECT ut.table_name, uc.constraint_name
FROM user_tables ut, user_constraints uc
WHERE ut.table_name = uc.table_name(+);
```

The (+) after uc.table_name makes the user_constraint table optional. The query returns all tables, and where there are no corresponding constraint records, Oracle supplies a null in the constraint name column.

Table Joins (Oracle9i and Higher)

Oracle9*i* Database introduces new table join syntax; this is the join syntax defined by the ANSI SQL:1992 standard. Join conditions may now be written in the FROM clause, making it easier to follow the logic of a query. In addition, the new syntax supports full outer joins, something not possible using the old syntax. Unless you need to maintain compatibility with old releases of Oracle, I strongly recommend using the new syntax.

Sample tables

Example queries in this section on SQL:1992 table joins are based on the following three tables:

```
SQL> SELECT *
  2  FROM course;

COURSE_NAME         PERIOD
--------------- ----------
Spanish I                1
Spanish 1                6
U.S. History             3
English II               4

SQL> SELECT *
  2  FROM enrollment;

COURSE_NAME         PERIOD STUDENT_NAME
--------------- ---------- ---------------
English II               4 Michael
Spanish I                1 Billy
Spanish I                6 Jessica
Spanish I                1 Jeff
English II               4 Jenny

SQL> SELECT *
  2  FROM student;

STUDENT_NAME         GRADE
--------------- ----------
Michael                  6
Billy                    3
Jessica                  1
Jeff                     1
Jenny                    8
```

Note that Jessica's enrollment record is without a matching COURSE record. She is registered for Spanish I (letter "I"), while the course is Spanish 1 (digit "1"). This becomes significant when performing an outer join and when using the USING clause.

Inner joins ("simple join")

Use the INNER JOIN keywords in the FROM clause to specify an inner join between the two tables. Use the ON clause to specify your join conditions. For example:

```
SELECT c.course_name, c.period, e.student_name
FROM course c INNER JOIN enrollment e
     ON c.course_name = e.course_name
        AND c.period = e.period;
```

Other clauses, such as WHERE and ORDER BY come after the FROM clause:

```
SELECT c.course_name, c.period, e.student_name
FROM course c INNER JOIN enrollment e
     ON c.course_name = e.course_name
        AND c.period = e.period
WHERE c.period < 9
ORDER BY c.period, c.course_name;
```

Join order

When joining more than two tables, use parentheses to control the join order. The following query joins COURSE and ENROLLMENT first, and then joins the table named STUDENT to the result:

```
SELECT c.course_name, c.period, s.student_name, s.grade
FROM (course c INNER JOIN enrollment e
        ON c.course_name=e.course_name
        AND c.period=e.period)
     INNER JOIN student s
     ON e.student_name=s.student_name;
```

If you omit parentheses, Oracle processes the joins from left to right. Unfortunately, moving parentheses around in SQL to change the join order is more difficult than moving parentheses around to change the order of a mathematical expression. The following query returns the same results as the previous one, because all joins are inner, but this time, the parentheses specify that the join between ENROLLMENT and STUDENT should logically come first:

```
SELECT c.course_name, c.period, s.student_name, s.grade
FROM course c INNER JOIN (enrollment e
    INNER JOIN student s
        ON e. student_name = s.student_name)
    ON c.course_name = e.course_name
        AND c.period = e.period;
```

Notice the new location of the ON clause between the COURSE and ENROLLMENT tables. It had to move from its previous location, just following ENROLLMENT, to its new location, following the closing parentheses. It can be a bit tedious to write a series of joins correctly using parentheses to specify anything other than a left-to-right join order.

Left and right outer joins

To perform an outer join of the type traditionally supported by Oracle, use either LEFT OUTER JOIN or RIGHT OUTER JOIN. Left and right outer joins are similar; the difference lies in the ordering of the tables in the FROM clause. The following query uses the old syntax to return all rows from COURSE together with any matching rows from ENROLLMENT:

```
SELECT c.course_name, c.period, e.student_name
FROM course c, enrollment e
WHERE c.course_name = e.course_name(+)
    AND c.period = e.period(+);
```

In this query, ENROLLMENT is considered the optional table because (+) is appended to each of that table's columns. The following two queries accomplish the same join using the new ANSI standard syntax:

```
SELECT c.course_name, c.period, e.student_name
FROM course c LEFT OUTER JOIN enrollment e
    ON c.course_name = e.course_name
        AND c.period = e.period;
```
"required" or
"mandatory"
table
on side of direction
word

```
SELECT c.course_name, c.period, e.student_name
FROM enrollment e RIGHT OUTER JOIN course c
    ON c.course_name = e.course_name
        AND c.period = e.period;
```
"mandatory"
table

Note the difference between the two queries. The first query lists the COURSE table first, while the second query lists the ENROLLMENT table first. A LEFT OUTER JOIN makes the left table the required table. A RIGHT OUTER JOIN makes the right table the required table. In both queries, ENROLLMENT is the optional table, and COURSE is the required table. Both queries return the same result.

Full outer joins

The *full outer join* represents a new capability in Oracle9*i* Database. A full outer join returns all rows from both tables. Where possible, rows from one table are matched with those from the other. In Oracle8*i* Database, you can simulate a full outer join using a UNION query:

```
SELECT c.course_name, c.period, e.student_name
FROM course c, enrollment e
WHERE c.course_name = e.course_name(+)
  AND c.period = e.period(+)
UNION
SELECT e.course_name, e.period, e.student_name
FROM enrollment e
WHERE NOT EXISTS (
   SELECT *
   FROM course c2
   WHERE c2.course_name = e.course_name
     AND c2.period = e.period
   );
```

To execute this UNION query, Oracle needs to execute each SELECT statement separately and then combine the results. You can potentially end up with two full table scans for each table. In Oracle9*i* Database, you can use FULL OUTER JOIN to do the same thing:

```
SQL> SELECT c.course_name, c.period, e.student_name
  2  FROM course c FULL OUTER JOIN enrollment e
  3     ON c.course_name = e.course_name
  4        AND c.period = e.period;
```

```
COURSE_NAME          PERIOD STUDENT_NAME
---------------- ---------- ----------------
English II                4 Michael
Spanish I                 1 Billy
Spanish I                 1 Jeff
English II                4 Jenny
Spanish 1                 6
U.S. History              3
                            Jessica
```

This query is easier to understand than the UNION query. It is also one SELECT statement and should execute more efficiently than the UNION query shown previously.

Specifying join conditions

Oracle9i Database supports three ways to specify join conditions: the ON, NATURAL, and USING clauses. The most general approach is to use the ON clause, in which you can specify any type of join condition. For example:

```
SELECT c.course_name, c.period, e.student_name
FROM course c FULL OUTER JOIN enrollment e
  ON c.course_name = e.course_name
     AND c.period = e.period;
```

This particular query is an *equi-join*; it looks for cases in which the corresponding columns from the two tables contain the same values. Because the names of the join columns are identical in the two tables, this join is also considered a *natural join*. Oracle supports the following shorthand syntax for natural joins:

```
SELECT course_name, period, e.student_name
FROM course c
     NATURAL FULL OUTER JOIN enrollment e;
```

Note that table aliases are not used for the join columns in the select list. In a natural join, Oracle recognizes only one version of each join column.

WARNING

Natural joins are dangerous! Use them only for queries you type in interactively.

Though NATURAL join syntax is convenient, you must exercise caution when using it. Consider what will happen if you code your programs using the NATURAL syntax and later add a column, UPDATE_TIMESTAMP, to each of your tables. This column is automatically included in all your joins, and your join queries will return erroneous results. I strongly recommend the USING clause over the NATURAL keyword.

The USING clause is another shortcut to performing an equi-join. The difference between USING and NATURAL is that with USING, you explicitly specify the join columns. Later changes to your tables won't alter the semantics of your queries. The following query uses USING to perform the same full outer join as in the previous two examples:

```
SQL> SELECT course_name, period, e.student_name
  2  FROM course c FULL OUTER JOIN enrollment e
  3  USING (course_name, period);

COURSE_NAME      PERIOD STUDENT_NAME
--------------- ---------- ---------------
English II            4 Michael
Spanish I             1 Billy
Spanish I             1 Jeff
English II            4 Jenny
Spanish 1             6
U.S. History          3
Spanish I             6 Jessica
```

Compare the results of this query with the results shown previously. Notice that Jessica's course name shows up in these results. That's because when USING or NATURAL is used, Oracle recognizes only one version of each join column and draws the value from whichever table it can.

Partition Outer Joins

Oracle Database 10g introduces a highly useful type of join called the *partition outer join*. This join type divides the rows from the optional table into partitions, or groups, based on a list of columns that you provide and repeats the outer join for each partition. Partition outer joins are useful for *data densification*, which involves filling in missing rows in a range.

Consider, for example, the problem of generating a list of project charges for the month of August 2004 for each combination of project, employee, and day. You might begin with a query such as this one:

```
SELECT project_id p_id, employee_id e_id,
       dollars_charged dollars, time_log_date log_date
FROM project_hours
WHERE time_log_date >=
        TO_DATE('1-Aug-2004','dd-mon-yyyy')
  AND time_log_date <
        TO_DATE('1-Sep-2004','dd-mon-yyyy')
ORDER BY project_id, employee_id, time_log_date;
```

A very quick look at the output shows that there are many "holes" in the results. There are many days on which employees have not billed time to a particular project. For example, this query's output shows that employee 101 billed time to project 1001 only once, on the first of the month:

```
    P_ID        E_ID    DOLLARS LOG_DATE
---------- ----------- ---------- ---------
    1001         101        507 01-AUG-04
    1001         105        605 15-AUG-04
    1001         107        135 02-AUG-04
...
```

There are many reasons why you might want your output to show 31 rows for employee 101 and project 1001, even if 30 of those rows showed that zero dollars were charged. You might, for example, be generating data for some kind of graph, such as a bar chart. The following query uses the new, partition outer join syntax to generate one billing record per

employee per project per day for the month of August 2004.
Pay particular attention to the highlighted lines:

```
WITH days_in_month AS
     (SELECT TO_DATE('1-Aug-2004',
                     'dd-mon-yyyy') + x day
      FROM pivot
      WHERE x BETWEEN 0 AND 30)
SELECT project_id p_id, employee_id e_id,
       NVL(dollars_charged, 0) dollars,
       dm.day log_date
FROM project_hours ph
     PARTITION BY (ph.project_id, ph.employee_id)
     RIGHT OUTER JOIN days_in_month dm
     ON ph.time_log_date = dm.day
WHERE dm.day >=
          TO_DATE('1-Aug-2004','dd-mon-yyyy')
  AND dm.day <
          TO_DATE('1-Sep-2004','dd-mon-yyyy')
ORDER BY ph.project_id, ph.employee_id,
         dm.day;
```

The results from this query are as follows:

```
     P_ID       E_ID    DOLLARS LOG_DATE
---------- ---------- ---------- ---------
      1001        101        507 01-AUG-04
      1001        101          0 02-AUG-04
      1001        101          0 03-AUG-04
      1001        101          0 04-AUG-04
...
```

Following are the key points to notice about this query:

- The WITH clause creates a result set named dm that
  contains 31 rows, one for each day in the month of
  August. This subquery could have been embedded into
  the main query's FROM clause. I factored it out here for
  clarity.

- The PARTITION BY clause specifies that the outer join
  between days_in_month (aliased as dm) and project_
  hours be done for each combination of project and
  employee. The dm table is the non-optional table, so the
  result will be one row per day from each partition of the
  join.

- The SELECT list references dm.day rather than ph.time_log_date. This is because ph.time_log_date will often be null as a result of the outer join.

- Similarly, the NVL function is applied to dollars_charged in the SELECT list, to ensure that any rows created by the outer join contain a zero rather than a null for the dollars charged. In this case, the absence of a row is tantamount to no charge.

- The WHERE and ORDER BY clauses reference dm.day rather than ph.time_log_date, because dm.day will never be null.

The first row of output shown for this example indicates a charge of 507 dollars and clearly represents a row that really does exist in project_hours. The following three rows that you see were created by the outer join. They are not present in my sample data. If you need to be certain whether the rows were originally present, you could include ph.time_log_date in the output. That column is part of the project_hours primary key and is not one of the PARTITION BY columns, so it will be null for new rows created by the outer join, and non-null otherwise.

One last note: partition outer joins will densify rows in each partition. However, they cannot be used to create new partitions. For example, without at least one project_hours row for employee 101 and project 1001 dated sometime during the month of August, you would not see that employee and project combination in the output from this section's partition outer join query.

TIP

For information on creating the pivot table used in this example, visit *http://gennick.com/pivot.html*. For another, somewhat more detailed example and explanation of partition outer joins, visit *http://gennick.com/partition.html*.

Summary Queries

The GROUP BY and HAVING clauses, together with Oracle's built-in aggregate functions, allow you to summarize the data returned by a query.

Using aggregate functions

Aggregate functions take data from multiple rows as input and return one summarized value. For example, the following query uses the COUNT function to return the number of tables you own:

```
SELECT COUNT(*)
FROM user_tables;
```

Oracle supports numerous aggregate functions. Some of the more commonly used such functions are:

AVG([DISTINCT | ALL] *value*)
    Returns the arithmetic mean of a set of values.

CORR(*value, value*)
    Returns the correlation coefficient (using Pearson's correlation) of a set of paired numbers.

COUNT([DISTINCT | ALL] *value*)
    Counts non-null values in a group.

MAX([DISTINCT | ALL] *value*)
    Returns the maximum of a set of values.

MEDIAN(*value*)
    Sorts a set of input values and returns the middle value. New in Oracle Database 10g.

MIN([DISTINCT | ALL] *value*)
    Returns the minimum of a set of values.

SUM([DISTINCT | ALL] *value*)
    Sums a set of numbers.

Used by themselves, these functions operate on the set of all values in a column returned by the query. Using GROUP BY, you can more narrowly define the sets of input values on which the functions operate.

Using GROUP BY

In addition to summarizing the entire results of a query, you can summarize the data for each distinct value in a column. For example, the following query returns the number of columns in each table you own:

```
SELECT ut.table_name, COUNT(utc.column_name)
FROM user_tables ut, user_tab_columns utc
WHERE ut.table_name = utc.table_name
GROUP BY ut.table_name
ORDER BY ut.table_name;
```

The next query extends the previous query and displays the number of columns in each table to which you have access. This time, the grouping results in one row for each distinct owner and table name combination:

```
SELECT at.owner, at.table_name, COUNT(atc.column_name)
FROM all_tables at, all_tab_columns atc
WHERE at.table_name = atc.table_name
GROUP BY at.owner, at.table_name
ORDER BY at.owner, at.table_name;
```

If you want the results of a GROUP BY query returned in any particular order, you must include an ORDER BY clause. However, an ORDER BY clause is not required. At times, it may appear that Oracle automatically sorts GROUP BY queries. It does, but only to a point. If you want the results sorted, you must include an ORDER BY clause.

Columns in the SELECT list of a GROUP BY query must be either listed in the GROUP BY clause or enclosed by one of the aggregate functions.

Restricting summarized results

You can use the HAVING clause to restrict the rows returned by a summary query to only the rows of interest. The HAVING clause functions just like the WHERE clause, except that the HAVING conditions are applied to the summarized results. For example, the following query returns a list of all tables for which you have not defined any indexes:

```
SELECT ut.table_name, COUNT(ui.index_name)
FROM user_tables ut, user_indexes ui
WHERE ut.table_name = ui.table_name(+)
GROUP BY ut.table_name
HAVING COUNT(ui.index_name) = 0;
```

This query works by first counting the number of indexes on each table and then eliminating those tables with nonzero counts.

Avoid placing conditions in the HAVING clause that do not test summarized values. Consider, for example, these two queries:

```
SELECT at.owner, at.table_name, COUNT(atc.column_name)
FROM all_tables at, all_tab_columns atc
WHERE at.table_name = atc.table_name
GROUP BY at.owner, at.table_name
HAVING at.owner <> 'SYS'
AND at.owner <> 'SYSTEM'
ORDER BY at.owner, at.table_name;

SELECT at.owner, at.table_name, COUNT(atc.column_name)
FROM all_tables at, all_tab_columns atc
WHERE at.table_name = atc.table_name
AND at.owner <> 'SYS'
AND at.owner <> 'SYSTEM'
GROUP BY at.owner, at.table_name
ORDER BY at.owner, at.table_name;
```

Both queries return the same result: a count of columns in each table except for those tables owned by SYS or SYSTEM. The second query, however, executes more efficiently because tables owned by SYS and SYSTEM are eliminated by the WHERE clause before the data is summarized.

Using ALL and DISTINCT

The aggregate functions ignore null values. By default, they include duplicate values. You can use the ALL and DISTINCT keywords to modify this behavior. For example:

```
SELECT COUNT(DISTINCT table_name)
FROM user_tab_columns;

SELECT COUNT(ALL table_name)
FROM user_columns;
```

The first query uses the DISTINCT keyword to count the number of tables. The second query uses the ALL keyword, representing the default behavior, to count the total number of columns defined for those tables.

Unions

SQL supports four union operators that allow you to take the results of two queries and combine them into one. These are listed in Table 1.

Table 1. SQL's union operators

Function	Description
UNION	Combines the results of two queries and then eliminates duplicate rows.
UNION ALL	Combines the results of two queries without eliminating duplicate rows.
MINUS	Takes the rows returned by one query and eliminates those that are also returned by another.
INTERSECT	Takes the results from two queries and returns only rows that appear in both.

The following example of a union query uses the MINUS operator to return a list of all tables for which you have not yet defined any indexes:

```
SELECT table_name
FROM user_tables
MINUS
SELECT DISTINCT table_name
FROM user_indexes
WHERE table_owner = USER
ORDER BY table_name;
```

cannot use a function in your sub query

The first query returns a list of all tables you own. The second query returns a list of all tables that are indexed. The MINUS union operation removes those indexed tables from the first list, leaving only the unindexed tables.

When two or more queries are unioned together, only one ORDER BY clause is allowed, which must be at the end. Only the rows returned as the final result are sorted.

TIP

To learn more about UNION operations, and especially to see some detailed examples, read "Is Yours A UNION Shop?" at *http://gennick.com/union.html*.

Partition Operations

When you're selecting data from partitioned tables and know that you want data from a specific partition only, you can explicitly specify the partition, or subpartition, to use. For example, specify a partition as follows:

```
SELECT *
FROM course PARTITION (2001_courses);
```

Specify a subpartition as follows:

```
SELECT *
FROM course SUBPARTITION (2001_qtr01_courses);
```

Be careful when using specific partition names in queries that you embed in programs, because those queries will fail if the specified partitions do not exist.

The pattern shown here for specifying partition and subpartition names can also be applied to INSERT, UPDATE, and DELETE statements.

Flashback Queries

Oracle supports syntax for *flashback queries*, which return rows as of some past point in time. The new syntax is specified between table names and their aliases in the FROM clause:

```
FROM table_name flashback table_alias

flashback ::= {as_of-clause | versions-clause}

as_of ::= AS OF {SCN system_change_number
                |TIMESTAMP timestamp}

versions ::= VERSIONS BETWEEN
                {SCN scn_start AND scn_end
                |TIMESTAMP ts_start AND ts_end}

scn_start ::= {system_change_number | MINVALUE}
scn_end ::= {system_change_number | MAXVALUE}

ts_start ::= {timestamp | MINVALUE}
ts_end ::= {timestamp | MAXVALUE}
```

Use the *as_of-clause* (Oracle9*i* Database Release 2 and higher) to return rows as of a specific, past point in time. Use the *versions-clause* (Oracle Database 10*g* and higher) to return all versions of selected rows between two system change numbers, or between two timestamps. Use the keywords MINVALUE and MAXVALUE when you want no lower limit, or no upper limit, respectively.

Following is an example of a flashback query, returning the list of employee records as of two days in the past:

```
SELECT e.employee_id, e.employee_name,
       e.employee_billing_rate
FROM employee AS OF TIMESTAMP
     SYSTIMESTAMP - INTERVAL '2' DAY e;
```

The database records the association between timestamp and system change number (SCN) at five-minute intervals. This history is maintained over a rolling, five-day period of database operation. You will receive an error if you attempt to flash back by timestamp to a point in time prior to the beginning of the current timestamp/SCN history. When you flash back by timestamp, the effect is that you will flash back to the SCN recorded at the five-minute interval just prior or equal to your timestamp.

TIP

You cannot apply flashback to temporary tables, external tables, clustered tables, or views.

Modeling Data

Oracle Database 10g features a powerful new clause, called MODEL, which enables spreadsheet-like calculations from a SELECT statement. It creates a multidimensional array in which cells can be referenced by dimension values.

MODEL Clause Syntax

The MODEL clause appears in the following position in a SELECT statement:

```
SELECT
...
GROUP BY
HAVING
MODEL model_clause
ORDER BY ...
```

The syntax of the MODEL clause is:

```
MODEL model_clause

model_clause ::= [options] [return]
   [reference_models] main_model

options ::= [{IGNORE | KEEP} NAV]
   [UNIQUE {DIMENSION | SINGLE REFERENCE}]
```

```
return ::= RETURN {UPDATED | ALL} ROWS

reference_models ::=
   reference_model [reference_model...]

reference_model ::= REFERENCE model_name
   ON (subquery) model_columns [options]

model_columns ::= [partition [alias]]
   DIMENSION BY (column[, column...])
   MEASURES (column[, column...])

partition ::= PARTITION BY (column[, column...])

column ::= {column_name | expression} [AS alias]

main_model ::= [MAIN model_name]
   model_columns [options] rules

rules ::=
   [RULES [UPSERT | UPDATE]
      [{AUTOMATIC | SEQUENTIAL} ORDER]]
   [ITERATE (count)
      [UNTIL (termination_condition)]]
   (rule[, rule...])

rule ::= [UPSERT | UPDATE] cell_reference
   [ordering] = expression

cell_reference ::=
   measure[multi_column_for_loop
           |dimension_indexes]

multi_column_for_loop ::=
   FOR (dimension[, dimension...])
   IN (dimension_values)

dimension_values ::= (
   {subquery | dimension_value
   [, dimension_value...]})

dimension_value ::= (literal[, literal...])

dimension_indexes ::= index[, index...]
```

```
index ::= {condition | expression
   |single_column_for_loop}

single_column_for_loop ::= FOR dimension
   {in_for_options | like_for_options}

in_for_options ::= IN ({subquery | literal
   [, literal...]})

like_for_options ::= [LIKE pattern]
   FROM start_literal TO end_literal
   {INCREMENT | DECREMENT} diff_literal

ordering ::= ORDER BY
   (order_column[, order_column...])

order_column ::= {expression | alias}
   [ASC | DESC] [NULLS FIRST | NULLS_LAST]
```

The parameters and clauses are as follows:

{IGNORE | KEEP} NAV

Specifies whether null or absent values (NAV) are
retained as nulls (KEEP) or are replaced with suitable
defaults (IGNORE): zero for numeric types, 1-Jan-2000
for date types, an empty string for character types, and
null for anything else.

UNIQUE {DIMENSION | SINGLE REFERENCE}

Specifies the scope within which the database ensures
that a given cell reference points to a unique data value.
Use DIMENSION to require that each *possible* cell reference, whether on the left or right side of a rule, represent
a single value. Use SINGLE REFERENCE to perform
that check only for those cell references that appear on
the right side of a rule.

RETURN {UPDATED | ALL} ROWS

Specifies whether all rows or only updated rows are
returned from model processing.

reference_model

Defines a reference model on which you cannot perform calculations, but which contains values that you can reference from within your main query.

model_name ON (*subquery*)

Specifies the name and rowsource for a reference model.

alias

Specifies an alias for a partition.

DIMENSION BY (*column*[, *column*...])

Specifies the dimensions for a model. Values from these columns represent the set of index values that are used to identify cells in the multidimensional addressing space.

MEASURES (*column*[, *column*...])

Specifies the values associated with each unique combination of dimensions (e.g., with each cell of the model).

PARTITION BY (*column*[, *column*...])

Splits a model into independent partitions based on the columns given. You cannot partition reference models.

main_model

Represents the model on which you perform work. Rows from your containing SELECT feed into this model, rules are applied, and the resulting rows are returned.

MAIN *model_name*

Begins the definition of the main model, and also gives that model a name.

RULES [UPSERT | UPDATE]

Specifies whether rules may both create new cells and update existing cells (UPSERT), or whether they may update existing cells (UPDATE) only. If you want your model to be able to create new rows in your result set, specify UPSERT, which is the default. You can also control this behavior on a rule-by-rule basis; see *rule* in the syntax.

{AUTOMATIC | SEQUENTIAL} ORDER

Specifies whether the optimizer determines the order in which rules are evaluated (AUTOMATIC), or whether rules are evaluated in the order in which you list them (SEQUENTIAL). The default is SEQUENTIAL.

ITERATE (*count*)

Requests that the entire set of rules be evaluated repeatedly, *count* times. The default is to evaluate the set of rules only once.

UNTIL (*termination_condition*)

Specifies a condition that, when met, causes iteration to cease. You must still specify a *count*, which serves as somewhat of a safeguard against infinite loops.

measure[...]

References one of the measures listed in the MEASURES clause. When you reference a measure, the square brackets are part of the syntax. You must specify all dimensions, either via a subquery or by listing them, and the specific value of the measure associated with those dimensions will be returned, or referenced.

multi_column_for_loop

Iterates a for-loop over multiple dimensions at one time. The easiest way to picture this is to think of a subquery from which each row represents a specific combination of dimensions.

dimension_indexes

Lists values, whether from columns or expressions, that collectively identify a unique cell in the model.

single_column_for_loop

Iterates a for-loop over one dimension.

IN ({*subquery* | *literal*[, *literal*...]})

Specifies whether the source of values for a for-loop is a subquery or a specific list of literal values.

LIKE *pattern*

>Allows you to insert dimension values into a pattern. Use a percent sign to mark the location at which you want dimension values to be inserted. For example, use FOR x LIKE 'A%B' FROM 1 TO 3 INCREMENT 1 to generate values such as 'A1B', 'A2B', 'A3B'.

FROM *start_literal* TO *end_literal*
{INCREMENT | DECREMENT} *diff_literal*

>Defines the starting and ending for-loop values, and also the difference between each subsequent value as the loop iterates from start to end.

ORDER BY (*order_column*[, *order_column*...])

>Imposes an order of evaluation with respect to the cells referenced from the left side of a rule. Use this clause if you want a rule to be applied to cells in order. Otherwise, you have no guarantee as to the order in which the rule is applied to the cells that it affects.

MODEL Clause Functions

Following is a list of functions that have been designed specifically for use in the MODEL clause:

CV( ) or CV(*dimension_column*)

>Returns the current value of a dimension column. May be used only on the right side of an expression in a rule. When the CV() form is used, the dimension column is determined implicitly based on the function call's position in a list of dimension values.

PRESENTNNV(*measure*[*dimension*, *dimension*...],
not_null, was_null)

>Returns either *not_null* or *was_null*, depending on whether the specified measure was null when model processing began. This function may be used only from the right side of a rule expression.

PRESENTV(*measure*[*dimension, dimension...*],
did_exist, didnt_exist)

Returns either *did_exist* or *didnt_exist*, depending on whether the specified measure existed when model processing began. This function may be used only from the right side of a rule expression. Be aware that whether a measure existed is a completely separate question from whether that measure was null.

ITERATION_NUMBER

Returns zero on the first iteration through the rules, 1 on the second iteration, and so forth. This is useful when you want to base rule calculations on the number of iterations.

MODEL Clause Example

The following SELECT statement retrieves all project_hours rows for the month of August 2004:

```
SELECT project_id p_id, employee_id e_id,
       dollars_charged dollars,
       time_log_date log_date
FROM project_hours
WHERE time_log_date >=
         TO_DATE('1-Aug-2004','dd-mon-yyyy')
   AND time_log_date <
         TO_DATE('1-Sep-2004','dd-mon-yyyy')
ORDER BY project_id, employee_id, time_log_date;
```

You can add a MODEL clause as follows:

```
SELECT pid p_id, eid e_id,
       dc dollars,
       tld log_date
FROM project_hours
WHERE time_log_date >=
         TO_DATE('1-Aug-2004','dd-mon-yyyy')
   AND time_log_date <
         TO_DATE('1-Sep-2004','dd-mon-yyyy')
MODEL
    DIMENSION BY (project_id pid,
        employee_id eid, time_log_date tld)
```

```
      MEASURES (dollars_charged dc)
      RULES ()
   ORDER BY pid, eid, tld;
```

The RULES clause in this example is empty, so the MODEL clause does not affect the results. Notice however, that the MODEL clause gives aliases to the column names involved, and that those aliases are what you must use in the SELECT list and ORDER BY clause.

The following MODEL clause partitions by project_id and employee_id, effectively creating a separate model for each combination of project and employee.

```
SELECT pid p_id, eid e_id,
       dc dollars,
       tld log_date
FROM project_hours
WHERE time_log_date >=
         TO_DATE('1-Aug-2004','dd-mon-yyyy')
   AND time_log_date <
         TO_DATE('1-Sep-2004','dd-mon-yyyy')
MODEL
   PARTITION BY (project_id pid, employee_id eid)
   DIMENSION BY (time_log_date tld)
   MEASURES (dollars_charged dc)
   RULES ()
ORDER BY pid, eid, tld;
```

This next MODEL clause uses two rules to densify the data, ensuring that each combination of employee and project is represented by one row for each day in the month of August 2004. Each rule applies to all partitions.

```
SELECT pid p_id, eid e_id,
       dc dollars,
       tld log_date
FROM project_hours
WHERE time_log_date >=
         TO_DATE('1-Aug-2004','dd-mon-yyyy')
   AND time_log_date <
         TO_DATE('1-Sep-2004','dd-mon-yyyy')
MODEL
   PARTITION BY (project_id pid, employee_id eid)
   DIMENSION BY (
```

```
      EXTRACT(DAY FROM time_log_date) dy)
   MEASURES (dollars_charged dc, time_log_date tld)
   RULES (
      dc[FOR dy FROM 1 TO 31 INCREMENT 1]
         = PRESENTV(dc[CV()], dc[CV()], 0),
      tld[FOR dy FROM 1 TO 31 INCREMENT 1]
         = DATE '2004-08-01' + CV(dy) - 1
   )
ORDER BY pid, eid, tld;
```

This data densification problem is the same that you saw ear-lier, under "Selecting Data" in the subsection on "Partition Outer Joins."

TIP

For a real-life example of how MODEL can be used in some cases to improve performance, see Anthony Molin-aro's article at *http://www.oreillynet.com/pub/a/network/2004/08/10/MODELclause.html*. For a more detailed dis-cussion of MODEL syntax, see my *Oracle Magazine* arti-cle: *http://www.oracle.com/technology/oramag/oracle/04-jan/o14tech_sql.html*, or see the Oracle Database 10g *SQL Reference*.

Inserting Data

Use the INSERT statement to add new rows to a table. In Oracle9i Database and higher, you have the ability to per-form direct path and multitable inserts. For the examples in this section, I've added a column to the COURSE table shown previously in the section on "Table Joins (Oracle9i and Higher)":

```
ALTER TABLE COURSE ADD (
   course_hours NUMBER DEFAULT 4);
```

Inserting One Row

To insert one row into a table, specify the list of columns for which you wish to insert a value and use the VALUES clause to specify values for the columns in your list:

```
INSERT INTO COURSE (course_name, period, course_hours)
VALUES ('French I', 5, DEFAULT);
```

The DEFAULT keyword is new in Oracle9i Database and is used in this query to explicitly request the default value for the course_hours column. You can use the NULL keyword, available in all releases of Oracle, to explicitly insert a null into a column.

You can omit the list of columns if you provide a value for each column in your table, and if you provide those values in the same order in which the columns are listed when you DESCRIBE the table:

```
INSERT INTO COURSE
VALUES ('French I', 5, DEFAULT);
```

I don't recommend this shortcut unless you are just typing in a one-off query interactively. It's safer to specify the column names.

Inserting the Results of a Query

Use the INSERT...SELECT...FROM syntax to insert the results of a query into a table. For example, the following INSERT statement creates a new row in the COURSE table for any currently undefined courses for which students are registered:

```
INSERT INTO COURSE (course_name, period)
SELECT DISTINCT course_name, period
FROM enrollment e
WHERE NOT EXISTS (
   SELECT *
   FROM course c
   WHERE c.course_name = e.course_name
     AND c.period = e.period
   );
```

When using INSERT...SELECT...FROM to populate a table with a large amount of data, you may be able to improve performance by doing a *direct path* insert. Use the APPEND hint for this (see "Using Optimizer Hints" under "Tuning SQL," later in this book). A direct path insert functions much like a direct path load: the database buffer cache is bypassed, and data is written directly to new extents in the datafiles.

Multitable Inserts (Oracle9i and Higher)

Multitable inserts are a new feature in Oracle9i Database; they allow you to insert the results of a SELECT query into several different tables at once. Write WHEN clauses into your INSERT statement in order to direct rows to the proper table.

The following INSERT statement uses Oracle9i Database's multitable insert functionality to do the following:

- Insert courses for period 6 into the table named COURSE_6.
- Insert courses for period 3 into the table named COURSE_3.
- Insert all other courses into the table named COURSE_OTHER:

```
INSERT ALL
WHEN (period=6) THEN
    INTO course_6 (course_name, period)
        values(course_name, period)
WHEN (period=3) THEN
    INTO course_3 (course_name, period)
        values(course_name, period)
ELSE
    INTO course_other (course_name, period)
        values(course_name, period)
SELECT course_name, period
FROM course;
```

The ALL keyword causes Oracle to check each row returned by the SELECT query against each WHEN clause. If a row satisfies more than one WHEN clause, it is inserted into more than one table. Use the FIRST keyword to limit inserts to only the first matching WHEN clause.

The previous INSERT statement illustrated a *conditional* multitable insert. Use an *unconditional* multitable insert to perform each INTO clause you specify. For example:

```
INSERT ALL
    INTO courses_taken (course_name)
        values (course_name)
    INTO students_registered (student_name)
        values (student_name)
SELECT course_name, student_name
FROM enrollment;
```

Note that regardless of whether you perform an unconditional or a conditional multitable insert, the target tables for each INTO clause do not need to be the same.

Updating Data

Use the UPDATE statement to modify column values in existing table rows.

Simple Updates

A simple UPDATE statement takes the following form:

```
UPDATE table_name
SET column_name = new_value,
    column_name = new_value,
    column_name = new_value,
    ...
WHERE selection_criteria;
```

For example, the following statement corrects a small problem with a course name; it changes the name to use an "I" (letter) instead of a "1" (digit):

```
UPDATE course
SET course_name = 'Spanish I'
WHERE course_name = 'Spanish 1';
```

Be careful with updates. If you omit the WHERE clause, your update will be applied to *all* rows in the table.

Noncorrelated Subqueries in the SET Clause

Rather than specify a new value in the SET clause for a column, you can specify a subquery that returns exactly one value (one column, one row). That value then becomes the new column value. For example:

```
UPDATE enrollment
SET period = (
        SELECT period
        FROM course
        WHERE course_name = 'English II'),
    course_name = (
        SELECT course_name
        FROM course
        WHERE course_name = 'English II'),
WHERE course_name = 'English II';
```

Setting the PERIOD and COURSE_NAME columns to their current values by way of a subquery doesn't make much sense. I did it only to show that you can use more than one subquery in an UPDATE statement.

Correlated Subqueries in the SET Clause

Subqueries in UPDATE statements are often more useful when they are correlated. A correlated subquery is one in which the row returned depends on the current row being updated. For example, the following UPDATE statement uses a correlated subquery to reset all periods in the enrollment table to values taken from the COURSE table:

```
UPDATE enrollment e
SET period = (
        SELECT MIN(period)
        FROM course c
        WHERE c.course_name = e.course_name);
```

Note the use of the table aliases c and e to qualify the column names in the WHERE clause. I used the MIN function in this case, because some courses (Spanish I, for example) are offered in more than one period.

When using correlated subqueries, you can specify multiple columns in your SET clause; just be sure to enclose them within parentheses:

```
UPDATE enrollment e
SET (course_name, period) = (
        SELECT course_name, period
        FROM course c
        WHERE c.course_name = e.course_name
          AND c.period = e.period);
```

This UPDATE statement, which serves only as a usage example, essentially uses a subquery to set course_name and period to their current values.

Deleting Data

Use the DELETE statement to delete rows from a table.

Simple Deletes

A simple DELETE statement takes the following form:

```
DELETE FROM table_name
WHERE selection_criteria
```

All rows meeting the selection criteria will be deleted. For example, to delete the sixth-period Spanish I course, specify:

```
DELETE FROM course
WHERE course_name = 'Spanish I'
  AND period = 6;
```

Be careful with DELETE statements. If you omit the WHERE clause, you will delete all rows from your table.

Deleting All Rows (TRUNCATE)

You can delete all rows from a table by issuing a DELETE without a WHERE clause:

```
DELETE FROM course;
```

Deleting all rows like this exacts a price. The deletion of each row must be logged to the database redo log, and a copy of each row to be deleted must be written to a rollback segment (or to an undo tablespace) in case the transaction is rolled back. A more efficient mechanism for deleting all rows from a table is the TRUNCATE statement:

```
TRUNCATE TABLE course;
```

The TRUNCATE statement requires only one short entry in the database redo log and generates no rollback or undo data. As a result, it is faster to truncate a table than it is to delete all rows using a DELETE statement. Beware, however, that you cannot roll back a TRUNCATE statement. Once you issue it, all the data in your table is gone for good.

By default, TRUNCATE deallocates all extents assigned to the table. If you wish, you can save the extents for later use:

```
TRUNCATE TABLE course REUSE STORAGE;
```

This resets the table's highwater mark so that it no longer contains any rows, but all existing extents remain allocated to the table. Retaining the extents can be helpful if you plan to reload the table.

Deleting Duplicate Rows

Occasionally, it is necessary to delete "duplicate" rows from a table. This need probably arises more often on test systems than on production systems. One approach to deleting duplicate rows is arbitrarily deleting all but the one with the lowest ROWID value:

```
DELETE FROM course
WHERE ROWID NOT IN (
   SELECT MIN(ROWID)
   FROM course
   GROUP BY course_name, period);
```

The GROUP BY clause in the subquery defines "duplicate" as two rows having the same course name and period. The subquery returns a list of ROWID values in which each value represents the minimum ROWID for a given combination of course name and period. Those rows are retained. The use of NOT IN results in all other rows being deleted.

Merging Data (Oracle9i and Higher)

A common data-processing problem is the need to take some data, decide whether it represents a new row in a table or an update to an existing row, and then issue an INSERT or UPDATE statement as appropriate. In the past, this has always been at least a two-step process, requiring two round-trips to the database. New in Oracle9i Database is the MERGE statement, which makes the process of inserting or updating easier and more efficient than before.

The general form of the MERGE statement is as follows:

```
MERGE INTO table
USING data_source
ON (condition)
WHEN MATCHED THEN update_clause
WHEN NOT MATCHED THEN insert_clause;
```

In this syntax, *data_source* can be a table, view, or query. The condition in the ON clause is what Oracle looks at to determine whether a row represents an insert or an update to the target table.

TIP

Beginning in Oracle Database 10g, you no longer need to include both the WHEN MATCHED and WHEN NOT MATCHED clauses.

Here is an example of a MERGE statement:

```
MERGE INTO course c
USING (SELECT course_name, period, course_hours
       FROM course_updates) cu
ON (c.course_name = cu.course_name
```

```
      AND c.period = cu.period)
WHEN MATCHED THEN
   UPDATE
   SET c.course_hours = cu.course_hours
WHEN NOT MATCHED THEN
   INSERT (c.course_name, c.period,
           c.course_hours)
   VALUES (cu.course_name, cu.period,
           cu.course_hours);
```

When processing this statement, Oracle reads each row from the query in the USING clause and looks at the condition in the ON clause. If the condition in the ON clause evaluates to TRUE, the row is considered to be an update to the COURSE_HOURS column. Otherwise, the row is considered a new row and is inserted into the COURSE table.

The following example shows the effects of the MERGE statement on the data in the COURSE table:

```
SQL> SELECT * FROM course;

COURSE_NAME          PERIOD COURSE_HOURS
---------------- ---------- ------------
Spanish I                 1
U.S. History              3
English II                4
French I                  5            4


SQL> SELECT * FROM course_updates;

COURSE_NAME          PERIOD COURSE_HOURS
---------------- ---------- ------------
Spanish I                 1            3
U.S. History              3            3
English II                4            3
French I                  5            3
Spelling                  6            2
Geography                 2            3


SQL> MERGE INTO course c
  2  USING (SELECT course_name, period,
  3         course_hours
  4         FROM course_updates) cu
  5  ON (c.course_name = cu.course_name
```

```
   6      AND c.period = cu.period)
   7   WHEN MATCHED THEN
   8     UPDATE
   9     SET c.course_hours = cu.course_hours
  10   WHEN NOT MATCHED THEN
  11     INSERT (c.course_name, c.period,
  12             c.course_hours)
  13     VALUES (cu.course_name, cu.period,
  14             cu.course_hours);
6 rows merged.

SQL> SELECT * FROM course;
```

COURSE_NAME	PERIOD	COURSE_HOURS
Spanish I	1	3
U.S. History	3	3
English II	4	3
French I	5	3
Spelling	6	2
Geography	2	3

Notice that the existing four rows in the COURSE table have had their COURSE_HOURS values updated and that two new rows have been added, all as the result of one statement.

Oracle Database 10g introduces a new DELETE subclause that allows you to delete rows from the target table based on conditions that exist after any updating has taken place. For example:

```
MERGE INTO course c
USING (SELECT course_name, period,
       course_hours
   FROM course_updates) cu
ON (c.course_name = cu.course_name
    AND c.period = cu.period)
WHEN MATCHED THEN
  UPDATE
  SET c.course_hours = cu.course_hours
  DELETE WHERE c.course_hours >= 3
WHEN NOT MATCHED THEN
  INSERT (c.course_name, c.period,
          c.course_hours)
  VALUES (cu.course_name, cu.period,
          cu.course_hours);
```

Execute this statement against the COURSE and COURSE_ UPDATES tables shown earlier in this section, and your final results will be as follows:

```
SQL> SELECT * FROM course;

COURSE_NAME         PERIOD COURSE_HOURS
--------------- ---------- ------------
Spelling                 6            2
Geography                2            3
```

The DELETE clause (highlighted in the preceding MERGE statement) deletes any courses that, *after having been updated*, represent more than three course hours. The DELETE affects only rows *updated* by the MERGE statement. The Geography course remains undeleted because it was *inserted* by the MERGE statement. Likewise, preexisting rows in the target table that are not touched by the MERGE operation are not candidates for deletion.

Transaction Management

Oracle implements several statements to help you manage transactions. By default, a transaction begins whenever you issue your first SQL statement. Once a transaction begins, you end it by doing one of the following:

- Issue a COMMIT
- Issue a ROLLBACK
- Issue a DDL statement

DDL statements (the ALTER and CREATE statements, for example) are special in that they implicitly end any open transaction. Thus, when issuing a DDL statement, it's possible to both begin and end a transaction with the same statement.

SET TRANSACTION

Use SET TRANSACTION explicitly to begin a transaction, especially when you want to specify transaction attributes such as isolation level.

```
SET TRANSACTION [attribute [,attribute...] ]
    NAME 'transaction_name';

attribute :=
    {READ {ONLY | WRITE}
    | ISOLATION LEVEL {SERIALIZABLE | READ COMMITTED}
    | USE ROLLBACK SEGMENT segment_name }
```

The READ COMMITTED isolation level is Oracle's default. It allows you to see changes made by other transactions as soon as they have been committed. Isolation-level SERIALIZABLE is more strict. With SERIALIZABLE, you can't modify any data that has been modified by others (but not committed before your transaction started). SERIALIZABLE also gives a consistent view of the data. You won't see changes committed by other users after your transaction begins. The following statement gives you a serializable transaction:

```
SET TRANSACTION
    ISOLATION LEVEL SERIALIZABLE
    NAME 'Jonathan''s Transaction';
```

READ ONLY transactions allow you to issue queries but not to change any data. READ ONLY transactions also provide read consistency. You don't see changes committed by other users during a READ ONLY transaction.

The USE ROLLBACK SEGMENT clause allows you to assign a transaction to a specific rollback segment. This is especially useful for large transactions, because you can assign those large transactions to a correspondingly large rollback segment. For example:

```
SET TRANSACTION
    USE ROLLBACK SEGMENT large_batch;
```

SAVEPOINT

SAVEPOINT allows you to established a named point in a transaction to which you can roll back if necessary.

```
SAVEPOINT savepoint_name;
```

COMMIT

COMMIT ends a transaction and makes permanent any changes made during the transaction.

```
COMMIT [WORK]
    [COMMENT 'text'
    |FORCE 'text'[, system_change_number]];
```

WORK is a "noise-word" and is usually omitted. The COMMENT clause allows you to associate a comment with a distributed transaction. The comment will be visible from the DBA_2PC_PENDING data dictionary view if the transaction is ever in doubt. The FORCE clause can manually commit an in-doubt, distributed transaction.

ROLLBACK

ROLLBACK is normally used to end a transaction and undo any changes made during the transaction. It can also undo changes back to a specified savepoint:

```
ROLLBACK [WORK]
    [TO [SAVEPOINT] savepoint_name
    |FORCE 'text'];
```

As in COMMIT, WORK is a noise-word and is rarely used. Use the FORCE clause to roll back an in-doubt, distributed transaction. Use TO savepoint_name to roll back to a specific savepoint.

Formatting Text Reports

SQL*Plus reports are columnar in nature. The program lets you define column headings and display formats for each column in a report. You may also define page headers and footers, page and line breaks, and summary calculations such as totals and subtotals.

Column Headings

Specify column headings using the HEADING clause of the COLUMN command:

```
COLUMN employee_name HEADING "Employee Name"
```

You can use either single or double quotes to enclose the heading text. The resulting heading looks like this:

```
Employee Name
-------------
```

To specify a multiline heading, use the vertical bar (|) character to specify the location of the line break. For example:

```
COLUMN employee_name HEADING "Employee|Name"
```

The resulting multiline heading looks like this:

```
Employee
Name
---------
```

Headings of text columns are aligned to the left. Headings of numeric columns are aligned to the right. Use the JUSTIFY clause to alter that behavior:

```
COLUMN employee_name HEADING "Employee|Name" -
   JUSTIFY RIGHT
COLUMN employee_name HEADING "Employee|Name" -
   JUSTIFY CENTER
```

Use SET HEADSEP to change the line-break character to something other than a vertical bar. Use SET UNDERLINE to change the underline character to something other than a hyphen.

Column Formats

You can specify display formats with the FORMAT clause of the COLUMN command. For numeric fields, format specifications can be quite detailed—controlling the length, the number of decimal places, and the punctuation used in the number. For text and date fields, you can control the column width and whether the column wraps. The later section "SQL*Plus Format Elements" shows how to format different types of data.

Page Width and Length

Page width is controlled by the SET LINESIZE command. The default width is 80 characters. You can change it—to 60 characters, for example—with this command:

```
SET LINESIZE 60
```

You can use the LINESIZE setting to center and right-justify page headers and footers.

Page length is controlled by the SET PAGESIZE command. The default is to print 24 lines per page (which includes the page header and page footer lines). The following command changes the page length to 50 lines:

```
SET PAGESIZE 50
```

When using SET MARKUP HTML ON to generate HTML output, PAGESIZE controls the number of HTML table rows that display before column headings are repeated; each row may display as one or more physical lines depending on how the browser window is sized.

Setting PAGESIZE to zero has a special meaning in SQL*Plus. A PAGESIZE of zero inhibits the display of page headers, page footers, and column headings. Pagination is turned off.

Page Headers and Footers

Define page headers and footers using the TTITLE and BTI-TLE commands. TTITLE, for top title, defines the page header. BTITLE, for bottom title, defines the page footer. The syntax is identical for both.

Defining a title

The following example defines a multiline page header with the company name on the left and the page number on the right:

```
TTITLE LEFT "My Company" CENTER "Current" -
RIGHT "Page" FORMAT 999 SQL.PNO SKIP 1 -
CENTER "Employee Listing" SKIP 4
```

The resulting title looks like this:

```
My Company        Current        Page    1
                Employee Listing
```

The final SKIP clause provides three blank lines between the page title and the column headers. The same clauses work in the BTITLE command to define page footers.

Getting the date into a title

To get the current date into a page title, you must:

1. Get the date into a user variable
2. Place the user variable into your BTITLE or TTITLE command

You can use the following commands in a SQL*Plus script to get the current date into a user variable:

```
SET TERMOUT OFF
COLUMN curdate NEW_VALUE report_date
SELECT TO_CHAR(SYSDATE,'dd-Mon-yyyy') curdate
FROM DUAL;
SET TERMOUT ON
```

After executing the commands shown here, the date will be in a user variable named REPORT_DATE. The following command places that value into a page footer:

```
BTITLE LEFT "Report Date: " report_date
```

You can use this same technique to retrieve other values from the database and place them in either a page header or a page footer.

Page Breaks

By default, SQL*Plus prints one blank line between each page of output. That blank line, added to the PAGESIZE setting, must equal the physical size of the pages in your printer.

The SET PAGESIZE command controls the number of lines SQL*Plus prints on a page. SET NEWPAGE controls the SQL*Plus action when a page break occurs. You can change the number of blank lines between pages using a command such as this:

```
SET NEWPAGE 10
```

You can tell SQL*Plus to display one form-feed character between pages by setting NEWPAGE to zero. For example:

```
SET NEWPAGE 0
```

Newer releases of SQL*Plus also allow SET NEWPAGE NONE, which eliminates both blank lines and form-feed characters between pages.

Report Breaks

The BREAK and COMPUTE commands define breaks and summary calculations for a report. BREAK also allows you to inhibit the display of repetitive column values.

The BREAK command

To eliminate repetitive column values, use the BREAK command as shown in this example:

```
SQL> BREAK ON owner

SQL> SELECT owner, table_name
  2  FROM all_tables
  3  ORDER BY owner, table_name;

OWNER       TABLE_NAME
==========  ===============
CTXSYS      DR$CLASS
            DR$DELETE
            DR$INDEX
DEMO        CUSTOMER
            DEPARTMENT
            EMPLOYEE
```

When you list a column in the BREAK command, SQL*Plus prints the value of the column only when it changes. It is very important that you remember to sort the query results on the same column.

You can also use the BREAK command to skip lines or to skip to a new page whenever a value changes. For example:

```
BREAK ON owner SKIP 1
BREAK ON owner SKIP PAGE
```

The first command prints a blank line whenever the owner changes. The second results in a page break each time the owner changes.

Multiple breaks may be specified for a report, but that's always done using just one command. The following example causes a page break to occur whenever an owner changes, and a blank line to be printed whenever the object type changes:

```
BREAK ON owner SKIP PAGE ON object_type SKIP 1
SELECT owner, object_type, object_name
FROM dba_objects
ORDER BY owner, object_type, object_name;
```

Before performing the break actions for a column, SQL*Plus first performs the break actions for all inner columns. In this case, a change in the owner field results in one skipped line and *then* a page break.

The COMPUTE command

The COMPUTE command tells SQL*Plus to compute summary values for groups of records. COMPUTE is always used in tandem with BREAK. For example, to compute the number of tables owned by each user, you can do the following:

```
BREAK ON owner
COMPUTE COUNT OF table_name ON owner
SELECT owner, table_name
    FROM dba_tables
ORDER BY owner, table_name;
```

SQL*Plus counts the number of table names for each distinct owner value and displays the results whenever a break occurs in the owner field.

You can compute summaries on multiple columns at once using multiple COMPUTE commands. The following example counts the number of objects of each type and sums the extent sizes for each object:

```
COMPUTE SUM OF bytes ON segment_name
COMPUTE COUNT OF segment_name ON segment_type
BREAK ON segment_type ON segment_name
SELECT segment_name, segment_type, bytes
    FROM user_extents
ORDER BY segment_type, segment_name;
```

Notice that the display order—the order used in the SELECT list—does not need to match the sort order or the break order. Also note that multiple summaries are defined using multiple COMPUTE commands, but multiple breaks are defined using just one BREAK command.

Formatting HTML Reports

Beginning with Oracle8*i* Database Release 2 (Version 8.1.6), you can use SQL*Plus to generate HTML pages. Instead of spooling a report to a printer, you can write it to an HTML file—for example, for viewing on your corporate intranet.

The Concatenation Approach

One approach to generating an HTML page with such data is to capture only the table containing the data, and to concatenate it with other HTML that you write yourself in order to generate a complete web page. The following script, for example, will generate a file named *middle.html* having an HTML table of employee data:

```
SET PAGESIZE 6
SET MARKUP HTML ON TABLE ""
COLUMN employee_id HEADING "ID"
COLUMN employee_name HEADING "Employee Name"
COLUMN employee_hire_date HEADING "Hire Date"
COLUMN employee_billing_rate -
      HEADING "Rate" FORMAT "$999.99"
SET TERMOUT OFF
SET FEEDBACK OFF
SPOOL middle.html
SELECT employee_id, employee_name,
       employee_hire_date,
       employee_billing_rate
FROM employee;
SPOOL OFF
```

Be sure to execute these commands from a script! If you type them interactively, SQL*Plus will also write the SELECT statement to the spool file. Assuming that you execute from a script file (using @ or START), the resulting *middle.html* file will contain a single, HTML table with all the query output:

```
<p>
<table>
<tr>
<th scope="col">
ID
</th>
<th scope="col">
Employee Name
</th>
<th scope="col">
Hire Date
</th>
<th scope="col">
```

```
Rate
</th>
</tr>
<tr>
<td align="right">
      101
</td>
<td>
Marusia Churai
</td>
<td>
15-NOV-61
</td>
<td align="right">
 $169.00
</td>
</tr>
...
```

There will be a leading <p> tag in the HTML spool file. SQL*Plus always writes that tag. This example sets PAGE-SIZE to 6, so you'll see a new heading in the table after every six rows of data. You can use a very large PAGESIZE if you prefer to see headings only once, at the beginning of the table.

SET TERMOUT OFF prevents query output from displaying on your screen while the script is running. SET FEED-BACK OFF prevents the "X rows selected" message from being written to the end of the spool file.

Now, if you have a file *first.html* with the following content:

```
<html>
<head>
<meta http-equiv="Content-Type"
content="text/html; charset=WINDOWS-1252">
<title>Employee Report</title>
<style type="text/css">
   table {border-collapse: collapse;
        width: 100%;}
   td {border: 2 solid black;}
   th {border: 2 solid black;}
</style>
<body>
<h1>Project Hours and Dollars Report</h1>
```

And if you have a *last.html* with these lines:

```
</body>
</html>
```

You can build a complete web page by concatenating everything together. On Unix or Linux, use *cat*:

```
cat first.html middle.html last.html >
    proj_hours_dollars.html
```

On Windows, use *type*:

```
type first.html middle.html last.html > full_page.html
```

The result from this example will be the simple page shown in Figure 5.

Figure 5. An HTML report

Generating Full Pages

The other approach to generating HTML reports from SQL*Plus is to generate complete HTML web pages. To that end, you'll want to use the SPOOL ON option for the SET MARKUP command:

```
SET MARKUP HTML ON SPOOL ON
```

The SPOOL ON option causes SQL*Plus to write <html>, <head>, and <body> tags before writing data from the query to the spool file, and to close those tags before closing the file. Thus, the result from running the script is a complete web page that you can immediately load into a browser.

Controlling page format

You can control page format using the HEAD, BODY, TABLE, and ENTMAP options for the SET MARKUP command—for example:

```
SET MARKUP -
   HTML ON -
   HEAD '<title>Employee Report</title> -
       <link href="emp_report.css" -
       rel="stylesheet" type="text/css"/>' -
   BODY "" -
   TABLE 'class="detail"' -
   ENTMAP OFF -
   SPOOL ON
```

The HEAD command in this example links the resulting web page to a stylesheet named *emp_report.css*. You can use such a stylesheet to control the way that browsers render the HTML that SQL*Plus generates. To that end, the TABLE option for this SET MARKUP command assigns a class to the detail table; that class can be referenced by CSS styles such as:

```
table.detail {background: #eeeeee; color: black}
```

Using ENTMAP OFF prevents SQL*Plus from translating < and > characters in the script's output stream to the HTML named character entities < and >. The net effect is that

---

you can then embed HTML tags into page headings (and footings):

```
TTITLE LEFT "<h1>The Fictional Company</h1>" -
       SKIP 1 -
       LEFT "<h2>Employee Report</h2>"
```

Rather than reference an external stylesheet, you also have the option of using SET MARKUP's HEAD option to embed CSS style definitions in your document (between <style> and </style> tags).

Page headings from TTITLE are written to their own table. There is no way to specify a class for the heading table, but you can control that table's format through the table style. There will be only one other table in a document, which holds the data. For that table, you *can* specify a class, which gives you a way to distinguish between the two tables.

TIP

When constructing headings for HTML reports, keep them simple. I have found it best to center everything or to left-align everything. You can use the keywords LEFT, CENTER, and RIGHT in a TTITLE for an HTML report, but the results, when rendered in HTML table cells, will often not look very good.

Another approach to page headings is to dispense with TTITLE altogether and use a PROMPT command to write out the heading that you want:

```
PROMPT <div class="top"> -
       <h1>The Fictional Company</h1> -
       <h2>Employee Report</h2> -
       </div> -
       <div class="bottom">
```

This approach depends on the setting ENTMAP OFF. The advantages here are twofold: headings aren't written within an HTML table, and headings won't repeat PAGESIZE rows.

Controlling column format

Unless you have ENTMAP OFF, there's not much you can do to control the rendering of the columnar, detail data in a report. With ENTMAP OFF, however, you can embed HTML tags into column headings. For example, you can associate each column heading with a class:

```
COLUMN employee_name HEADING -
"<p class=left>Employee Name</p>" -
FORMAT A40

COLUMN employee_billing_rate -
HEADING "<p class=right>Rate</p>" -
FORMAT 9,999.99
```

The classes left and right that you see in this example can be used to cause headings for character columns to display flush left, and headings for numeric columns to display flush right:

```
p.left {text-align: left}
p.right {text-align: right}
```

When you place HTML markup in text column headings, take care to format each column widely enough to accommodate its heading markup. I specified FORMAT A40 for employee_name to allow for up to 40 characters in the <p> tag. Were I to specify FORMAT A9, my heading text would be truncated to 9 characters, with the result that the incomplete tag <p class= would be written to my HTML file.

TIP

I have not experienced truncation problems with headings of numeric columns.

Tuning SQL

SQL*Plus can help you tune SQL statements. You can use SQL's EXPLAIN PLAN facility to get the execution plan for a statement into a table. You can then query that table using

---

SQL*Plus to display that plan. If you don't like the plan Oracle is using, you can add optimizer hints to your SQL statement that specify how you want the statement to be executed.

Creating the Plan Table

Before you can use the EXPLAIN PLAN statement, you need to create a plan table to hold the results. Oracle provides a script named *utlxplan.sql* to create the plan table. You'll find it in your *$ORACLE_HOME/rdbms/admin* directory. Execute the script as follows:

```
SQL> @$ORACLE_HOME/rdbms/admin/utlxplan
Table created.
```

Windows users, refer to the Oracle home directory as follows:

```
@%ORACLE_HOME%/rdbms/admin/utlxplan
```

In particular, note the bracketing of ORACLE_HOME by percent signs (%).

The resulting table, PLAN_TABLE, looks like this:

Name	Null?	Type
STATEMENT_ID		VARCHAR2(30)
PLAN_ID		NUMBER
TIMESTAMP		DATE
REMARKS		VARCHAR2(4000)
OPERATION		VARCHAR2(30)
OPTIONS		VARCHAR2(255)
OBJECT_NODE		VARCHAR2(128)
OBJECT_OWNER		VARCHAR2(30)
OBJECT_NAME		VARCHAR2(30)
OBJECT_ALIAS		VARCHAR2(65)
OBJECT_INSTANCE		NUMBER(38)
OBJECT_TYPE		VARCHAR2(30)
OPTIMIZER		VARCHAR2(255)
SEARCH_COLUMNS		NUMBER
ID		NUMBER(38)
PARENT_ID		NUMBER(38)
DEPTH		NUMBER(38)
POSITION		NUMBER(38)

COST	NUMBER(38)
CARDINALITY	NUMBER(38)
BYTES	NUMBER(38)
OTHER_TAG	VARCHAR2(255)
PARTITION_START	VARCHAR2(255)
PARTITION_STOP	VARCHAR2(255)
PARTITION_ID	NUMBER(38)
OTHER	LONG
DISTRIBUTION	VARCHAR2(30)
CPU_COST	NUMBER(38)
IO_COST	NUMBER(38)
TEMP_SPACE	NUMBER(38)
ACCESS_PREDICATES	VARCHAR2(4000)
FILTER_PREDICATES	VARCHAR2(4000)
PROJECTION	VARCHAR2(4000)
TIME	NUMBER(38)
QBLOCK_NAME	VARCHAR2(30)

The columns in the plan table vary from one release of Oracle to the next. This version of the plan table is from Oracle Database 10g Release 1 (10.1.0.2.0).

TIP

Beginning in Oracle Database 10g, the PLAN_TABLE is automatically created for you, as a global temporary table, when you execute your first EXPLAIN PLAN statement.

Explaining a Query

Use the EXPLAIN PLAN statement to get the execution plan for a SQL statement. Oracle places the execution plan into the plan table you've created.

EXPLAIN PLAN syntax

The syntax for EXPLAIN PLAN looks like this:

```
EXPLAIN PLAN
        [SET STATEMENT_ID = 'statement_id']
        [INTO table_name]
        FOR statement;
```

Here are the parameters:

statement_id
> Identifies the query you are explaining and is stored in the STATEMENT_ID field of the plan table records. This defaults to null.

table_name
> The name of the plan table; defaults to PLAN_TABLE.

statement
> The SELECT, INSERT, UPDATE, or DELETE statement to be explained.

EXPLAIN PLAN example

First, delete any existing plan table records with the statement ID you wish to use. For example:

```
DELETE FROM plan_table
WHERE statement_id = 'HOURS_BY_PROJECT';
```

Insert the EXPLAIN PLAN statement at the front of the SQL statement you are interested in explaining, then execute the resulting, longer statement. For example:

```
EXPLAIN PLAN
SET STATEMENT_ID = 'HOURS_BY_PROJECT'
FOR
SELECT employee_name, project_name,
       SUM(hours_logged)
FROM employee, project, project_hours
WHERE employee.employee_id
        = project_hours.employee_id
    AND project.project_id
        = project_hours.project_id
GROUP BY employee_name, project_name;
```

Your next step is to query the plan table for the results.

Using DBMS_XPLAN

Beginning in Oracle9*i* Database Release 2, you can use the DBMS_XPLAN package to display an execution plan that you have explained to the plan table. Here's an example:

```
SET LINESIZE 132

SELECT *
FROM TABLE(DBMS_XPLAN.DISPLAY(
             'PLAN_TABLE','HOURS_BY_PROJECT','TYPICAL')
        );
```

Figure 6 shows the output from this query, which won't otherwise fit within the margins of this book.

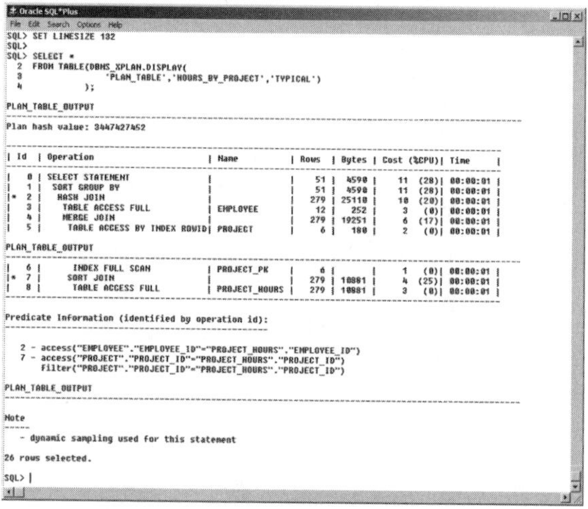


```
SQL> SET LINESIZE 132
SQL>
SQL> SELECT *
  2  FROM TABLE(DBMS_XPLAN.DISPLAY(
  3               'PLAN_TABLE','HOURS_BY_PROJECT','TYPICAL')
  4          );

PLAN_TABLE_OUTPUT
--------------------------------------------------------------------------------
Plan hash value: 3447427452

---------------------------------------------------------------------------------------------
| Id  | Operation                      | Name          | Rows  | Bytes | Cost (%CPU)| Time     |
---------------------------------------------------------------------------------------------
|   0 | SELECT STATEMENT               |               |    51 |  4590 |    11  (28)| 00:00:01 |
|   1 |  SORT GROUP BY                 |               |    51 |  4590 |    11  (28)| 00:00:01 |
|*  2 |   HASH JOIN                    |               |   279 | 25110 |    10  (20)| 00:00:01 |
|   3 |    TABLE ACCESS FULL           | EMPLOYEE      |    12 |   252 |     3   (0)| 00:00:01 |
|   4 |    MERGE JOIN                  |               |   279 | 19251 |     6  (17)| 00:00:01 |
|   5 |     TABLE ACCESS BY INDEX ROWID| PROJECT       |     6 |   180 |     2   (0)| 00:00:01 |

PLAN_TABLE_OUTPUT
--------------------------------------------------------------------------------
|   6 |      INDEX FULL SCAN           | PROJECT_PK    |     6 |       |     1   (0)| 00:00:01 |
|*  7 |     SORT JOIN                  |               |   279 | 10881 |     4  (25)| 00:00:01 |
|   8 |      TABLE ACCESS FULL         | PROJECT_HOURS |   279 | 10881 |     3   (0)| 00:00:01 |
---------------------------------------------------------------------------------------------

Predicate Information (identified by operation id):
---------------------------------------------------

   2 - access("EMPLOYEE"."EMPLOYEE_ID"="PROJECT_HOURS"."EMPLOYEE_ID")
   7 - access("PROJECT"."PROJECT_ID"="PROJECT_HOURS"."PROJECT_ID")
       filter("PROJECT"."PROJECT_ID"="PROJECT_HOURS"."PROJECT_ID")

PLAN_TABLE_OUTPUT
--------------------------------------------------------------------------------

Note
-----
   - dynamic sampling used for this statement

26 rows selected.

SQL> |
```

Figure 6. An execution plan as displayed by DBMS_XPLAN

The three parameters to the DBMS_XPLAN.DISPLAY function are:

table_name

Don't forget to specify your plan table's name as upper-case, unless you truly have a mixed- or lowercase plan table name.

statement_ID

This is the ID you specified in your EXPLAIN PLAN statement. Use NULL if you did not specify a statement ID.

format_keyword

This keyword describes how much detail you wish to see. It will ordinarily be one of the following, in increasing order of detail: BASIC, TYPICAL, or ALL. TYPICAL is the default. You may also use SERIAL in cases in which you want TYPICAL output, but without any information about parallel operations.

Oracle breaks query execution down into a series of nested steps, each of which feeds data up to a parent step. The ultimate parent is the query itself, the output of which is returned to the application.

Querying the Plan Table

If it's available, DBMS_XPLAN is by far the most convenient method for displaying an execution plan. However, you can also query the plan table yourself. You'll need to do that in older releases of Oracle. One possible query to display execution plan output looks like this:

```
SELECT LPAD(' ', 2*(level-1)) ||
       operation || ' ' || options
       || ' ' || object_name || ' ' ||
       DECODE(id, 0, 'Cost = ' || position)
       "Query Plan"
FROM plan_table
START WITH id = 0 AND statement_id
              = 'HOURS_BY_PROJECT'
CONNECT BY prior id = parent_id
       AND statement_id = 'HOURS_BY_PROJECT';
```

The result of this query, which uses CONNECT BY and the level pseudocolumn to nest steps under their parents, is a report showing the steps in the execution plan:

```
Query Plan
-----------------------------------------
SELECT STATEMENT    Cost = 7
  SORT GROUP BY
    HASH JOIN
      HASH JOIN
        TABLE ACCESS FULL EMPLOYEE
        TABLE ACCESS FULL PROJECT_HOURS
      TABLE ACCESS FULL PROJECT
```

The cost for one execution plan can be interpreted only relative to another. For example, a query with a cost of 14 requires twice the I/O and CPU resources of a query with a cost of 7.

WARNING

Statistics are required to compute a cost. Out-of-date statistics result in an inaccurate cost.

The innermost execution plan steps generally return a set of database ROWIDs. These ROWIDs then feed operations that may, in turn, feed other operations. Sometimes an operation requires two sets of ROWIDs. An example of this is the HASH JOIN operation in the preceding execution plan, which requires ROWIDs from full scans of all the rows in the EMPLOYEE and PROJECT_HOURS tables.

Many execution plan operations are understandable, or at least somewhat guessable, from their names alone, especially when you factor in your knowledge of the results you are requesting via your query. You can find full descriptions of execution plan operations in the *Oracle Database Performance Tuning Guide*.

Using Optimizer Hints

Rather than allow Oracle to have total control over how a query is executed, you can provide specific directions to the optimizer through the use of hints. A *hint*, in Oracle, is an optimizer directive that is embedded in a SQL statement in the form of a comment. For example, here is a query with an optimizer hint telling Oracle to do a full table scan:

```
SELECT /*+ FULL(employee) */
       employee_id,
       employee_name,
       employee_billing_rate
FROM employee
WHERE employee_name = 'Jenny Gennick';
```

The hint in this case is FULL(employee) telling Oracle to do a full table scan of the employee table. Oracle will honor this hint and perform a full table scan even if there happens to be an index on the employee name field.

TIP

Knowing which execution plan is optimal, and thus which hints to apply to a given statement, is, of course, the crux of any SQL tuning problem. For help in this important area, I can do no better than to point you towards Dan Tow's excellent book, *SQL Tuning* (O'Reilly). Dan's book is the only one I've ever seen that provides a repeatable and determinant methodology for finding the optimal, or near-optimal, execution plan. I highly recommend his book.

Hints must be in a comment of the form /*+...*/. This comment must follow the SQL keyword that begins the statement.

If you make a mistake specifying a hint, it will be treated as a comment. You won't get any error message. Whenever you use a hint, you should do an EXPLAIN PLAN before and after applying the hint to ensure that it is being interpreted and applied as you intend.

The following subsections describe hint query blocks and various categories of optimizer hints. Only the most commonly used hints are shown here.

Hint query blocks

Oracle Database 10g introduces a new, *query block* syntax for use in hints. When you have a statement, such as a SELECT, that consists of a main statement and one or more subqueries, each statement and subquery is a query block. The new query block syntax lets you refer to those query blocks by name from a hint.

You can name the query blocks in a statement using the QB_NAME hint. The statement in the following example contains two query blocks that are given the names main and sub, respectively. The two FULL hints use query block names to fully qualify their respective table references, with the end result that both instances of employee are accessed via a full table scan.

```
SELECT /*+ QB_NAME(main) FULL(@main e1)
           FULL(@sub e2) */
       e1.employee_name, employee_hire_date
FROM employee e1
WHERE EXISTS (
   SELECT /*+ QB_NAME(sub) */
          e2.employee_id
   FROM employee e2
   WHERE employee_hire_date >=
         TO_DATE('1-Jan-2000','dd-mon-yyyy')
     AND e1.employee_id = e2.employee_id);
```

If you don't name the query blocks in a statement, Oracle will generate query block names for you. To see those automatically generated names, run an EXPLAIN PLAN on your statement followed by a query using the ALL option of DBMS_XPLAN.DISPLAY:

```
SELECT PLAN_TABLE_OUTPUT
FROM TABLE(DBMS_XPLAN.DISPLAY
              (NULL, NULL, 'ALL'));
```

Optimizer goal hints

Optimizer goal hints allow you to influence the optimizer's overall goal when formulating an execution plan:

ALL_ROWS
> Produces an execution plan that minimizes resource consumption. Obsolete in Oracle Database 10*g*.

FIRST_ROWS and FIRST_ROWS(*num*)
> Produces an execution plan that gets to the first row, or to the first *num* rows, as fast as possible. FIRST_ROWS(*num*) is new in Oracle9*i* Database.

CHOOSE
> Uses the cost-based optimizer if statistics are present for at least one of the tables referenced in a query. Obsolete in Oracle Database 10*g*.

RULE
> Uses the rule-based optimizer. Obsolete in Oracle Database 10*g*.

Access method hints

Access method hints allow you to control the manner in which Oracle accesses data:

FULL(*table_name*)
FULL(@*block table*)
> Does a full table scan of the specified table.

INDEX(*table_name* [*index_name* ...])
INDEX(@*block table* [*index...*])
> Accesses the specified table via an index scan. Optionally, you may specify a list of indexes from which to choose. You may also use INDEX_ASC and INDEX_DESC to explicitly specify an ascending or descending scan, respectively.

INDEX_JOIN(*table_name* [*index_name* ...])
INDEX_JOIN(@*block table* [*index...*])

Rather than access the table, joins two or more of the table's indexes to retrieve the data required by the query. The indexes must collectively contain all columns referenced by the query. New in Oracle9*i* Database.

NO_INDEX (*table_name* [*index_name* ...])
NO_INDEX (@*block table* [*index...*])

Disallows the use of specified indexes on a table. If no indexes are specified, none of the table's indexes may be used.

Join order hints

Join order hints allow you to exercise some control over the order in which tables are joined:

FACT(*table*)
FACT(@*block table*)

Indicates that a table should be considered a fact table in a star query. New in Oracle Database 10*g*.

LEADING(*table_name*)

Makes the specified table the first table in the join order. New in Oracle9*i* Database. The ORDERED hint overrides LEADING.

NO_FACT(*table*)
NO_FACT(@*block table*)

Indicates that a table is not a fact table. New in Oracle Database 10*g*.

NO_STAR_TRANSFORMATION
NO_STAR_TRANSFORMATION(@*block*)

Prevents transformation into a star query. New in Oracle Database 10*g*.

ORDERED

Joins tables left to right in the same order in which they are listed in the FROM clause. New in Oracle Database 10*g*.

STAR

Uses a star query execution plan, if at all possible. Deprecated in Oracle Database 10g. Use STAR_TRANSFOR-MATION instead.

STAR_TRANSFORMATION
STAR_TRANSFORMATION(@block)

Tells Oracle to transform the query into a star query, if possible, and then to use the best plan for such a query. This can work only if there are at least three tables being joined and if the largest table has a concatenated index on columns that reference the two smaller tables. The two smaller tables are joined first, and then a nested-loop join retrieves the required rows from the largest table.

Join operation hints

Join operation hints allow you to control the manner in which two tables are joined:

USE_NL(table [*table...*])
USE_NL(@*block table* [*table...*])

Joins two tables using an outer loop to read one table and an inner loop to read all corresponding rows from the other table. This is known as a *nested-loops join*; it generally begins to return results most quickly, but overall may take the most time to execute. Specify the inner table in the hint. Specify multiple tables if you wish to affect multiple joins.

USE_MERGE(*table* [*table...*])
USE_MERGE(@*block table* [*table...*])

Performs a join on a table (or tables) by separately sorting that table's rows on the join key, also sorting the other rowset's rows on the same join key, and then reading through both resulting rowsets to merge the two rowsets.

USE_HASH(*table* [*table*...])
USE_HASH(@*block table* [*table*...])

Performs a hash join on the specified table (or tables). Creates a hash table in memory using the join key values from the smaller of the two rowsets (or tables) to be joined. It then scans the larger table, applying the same hash function to its join key columns. Hash joins may be used only for equi-joins (in which the = operator is used).

Query transformation hints

A single query can sometimes be expressed in more than one way. Oracle will sometimes rewrite your queries to enable the use of a more efficient execution plan. Query transformation hints allow you to control how, or even whether, such rewriting takes place:

MERGE
MERGE(*view*)
MERGE(@*block*)
MERGE(@*block view*)

Merges a view into a query.

NO_MERGE
NO_MERGE(*view*)
NO_MERGE(@*block*)
NO_MERGE(@*block view*)

Prevents views from being merged into a query. Use in a view's SELECT statement.

NO_REWRITE
NO_REWRITE(@*block*)

Prevents the use of materialized views. Prior to Oracle Database 10*g*, this hint was NOREWRITE, with no underscore, and the @*block* syntax was not supported.

REWRITE
REWRITE(*view* [*view*...])
REWRITE(@*block view* [*view*...]])
> Forces the use of materialized views where possible, regardless of cost. If you specify one or more materialized view names, only those views are considered for use.

USE_CONCAT
> Turns a query with OR conditions into two or more queries unioned together with a UNION ALL. This is known as *OR-expansion*. Use the NO_EXPAND hint to prevent OR-expansion.

Miscellaneous hints

Here are two useful miscellaneous hints:

APPEND
> Don't attempt to reuse any free space that may be available in any extents currently allocated to the table. Instead, add rows above the current highwater mark. Applies only to INSERT statements and has the same result as doing a direct path load using SQL*Loader. Use NOAPPEND to explicitly request that existing free space be reused. APPEND is the default behavior for parallel inserts; otherwise, NOAPPEND is the default behavior.

ORDERED_PREDICATES
> Causes predicates to be evaluated in the order in which you specify them in a WHERE clause. Unlike the other hints, you place this hint into the WHERE clause following the WHERE keyword. Deprecated in Oracle Database 10g.

SQL*Plus Format Elements

The COLUMN, ACCEPT, SET NUMBER, TTITLE, BTITLE, REPHEADER, and REPFOOTER commands allow you to control data formats using what is called a format specification. A *format specification* is a string of characters that tells SQL*Plus exactly how to format a number, date, or text string when it is displayed.

Formatting Numbers

Table 2 shows the format elements that may be used when formatting numeric output.

Table 2. Numeric format elements

Format element	Function
$	Includes a leading dollar sign in the output.
,	Places a comma in the output.
.	Marks the location of the decimal point.
0	Marks the spot at which you want to begin displaying leading zeros.
9	Represents a digit in the output.
B	Forces zero values to be displayed as blanks.
C	Marks the place where you want the ISO currency indicator to appear. For U.S. dollars, this is USD.
D	Marks the location of the decimal point.
DATE	Causes SQL*Plus to assume that the number represents a Julian date and to display it in MM/DD/YY format.
EEEE	Causes SQL*Plus to use scientific notation to display a value. You must use exactly four Es, and they must appear at the right end of the format string.
FM	Prefix: removes any leading or trailing blanks from the return value.
G	Places a group separator (usually a comma) in the output.
L	Marks the place where you want the local currency indicator to appear. For U.S. dollars, this is the dollar sign character.
MI	Adds a trailing negative sign to a number and may be used only at the end of a format string.
PR	Causes negative values to be displayed within angle brackets. For example, -123.99 is displayed as <123.99>.

Table 2. Numeric format elements (continued)

Format element	Function
RN	Allows you to display a number using Roman numerals. An uppercase RN yields uppercase Roman numerals, while a lowercase r n yields lowercase Roman numerals. Numbers displayed as Roman numerals must be integers and must be between 1 and 3,999, inclusive.
S	Adds a + or - sign[a] to the number and may be used at either the beginning or end of a format string.
TM	Prefix: returns a number using the minimum number of characters. TM stands for "text minimum." Follow TM with one 9 if you want a regular, decimal notation (the default) to be used. Follow TM with one E if you want scientific notation to be used.
U	Results in a Euro symbol being placed at the specified location. The NLS_DUAL_CURRENCY parameter actually controls the character returned by this format element.
V	Displays scaled values. The number of digits to the right of the V indicates how many places to the right the decimal point is shifted before the number is displayed.
X	Returns a number in hexadecimal value. You can precede this element with 0s in order to return leading zeros, or with FM in order to trim leading and trailing blanks. X cannot be used in combination with any other format elements.

[a] SQL*Plus always allows for a sign somewhere when you display a number. The default is for the sign to be positioned to the left of the number and to be displayed only when the number is negative. Positive numbers have a blank space in the leftmost position.

Table 3 contains several examples illustrating the use of the various format elements.

Table 3. Numeric format examples

Value	Format	Result
123	9999	123
1234.01	9,999.99	1,234.01
23456	$999,999.99	$23,456.00

Table 3. Numeric format examples (continued)

Value	Format	Result
1	0999	0001
1	99099	001
-1000.01	9,999.99mi	1,000.01-
1001	S9,999	+1,001
-1001	9,999PR	<1,001>
1001	9,999PR	1,001

Formatting Character Strings

Character strings are formatted using only one element. That element is "A", and it is followed by a number specifying the column width in terms of characters. For example:

```
SQL> COLUMN a FORMAT A40

SQL> SELECT 'An apple a day keeps the doctor away.' A
  2    FROM dual;

A
----------------------------------------
An apple a day keeps the doctor away.
```

By default, longer text values are wrapped within the column. You can use the WORD_WRAPPED, WRAPPED, and TRUNCATED parameters of the COLUMN command to control whether and how wrapping occurs. For example:

```
SQL> COLUMN a FORMAT A18 WORD_WRAPPED

SQL> SELECT 'An apple a day keeps the doctor away.' A
  2    FROM dual;

A
------------------
An apple a day
keeps the doctor
away.
```

When text columns wrap to multiple lines, SQL*Plus prints a blank line called a *record separator* following the record. Use SET RECSEP OFF to prevent that behavior.

When used with the ACCEPT command, a character format defines the maximum number of characters SQL*Plus will accept from the user.

Formatting Dates

The date format elements in Tables 1–4 may be used with Oracle's built-in TO_CHAR function to convert date values to character strings. For example:

```
SQL> SELECT TO_CHAR(SYSDATE,
  2 'dd-Mon-yyyy hh:mi:ss PM')
  3    FROM dual;

TO_CHAR(SYSDATE,'DD-MON
-----------------------
13-Dec-2001 09:13:59 PM
```

When used with the ACCEPT command, a date format string requires the user to enter a date in the format specified. Table 4 contains a list of date format elements.

Table 4. Date format elements

Format element	Function
-/,.;:	Punctuation to be included in the output.
AD or A.D. BC or B.C.	AD, A.D., BC, or B.C. indicator included with the date.
AM or A.M. PM or P.M.	AM, A.M., PM, or P.M. printed, whichever applies given the time in question.
CC	The century number—20 for years 1900 through 1999. See SCC.
D	The number of the day of the week—1 through 7.
DAY	The full name of the day.
DD	The day of the month.
DDD	The day of the year.

```
select to-char(systimestamp, 'ss.ff3')
       from dual;
```

Table 4. Date format elements (continued)

Format element	Function
DL	Returns a date in a *long-date* format, which depends on NLS_TERRITORY and NLS_LANGUAGE. May be combined only with TS.
DS	Returns a date in a *short-date* format, which depends on NLS_TERRITORY and NLS_LANGUAGE. May be combined only with TS.
DY	The abbreviated name of the day.
E	The abbreviated era name. Valid only for Japanese, Imperial, ROC Official, and Thai Buddha calendars.
EE	The full era name. See E.
FF FF1..FF9	The fractional seconds. Valid only for TIMESTAMP types. Beginning with Oracle Database 10*g*, you may use FF1..FF9 to specify the number of fractional digits you desire. *IF stored this way*
FM	Suppresses extra blanks and zeros in the character string representation of a date. For example, use 'FMMonth DD' to get 'July 4' rather than 'July 4'.
FX	Requires exact pattern matching between data and format model. (FX stands for Format eXact.)
HH	The hour of the day on a 12-hour clock.
HH12	The hour of the day on a 12-hour clock.
HH24	The hour of the day on a 24-hour clock.
I	The last digit of the year number.
IW	The ISO week number, which can be 1–53. See IYYY.
IY	The last two digits of the ISO year number.
IYY	The last three digits of the ISO year number.
IYYY	The four-digit ISO year. The ISO year begins on Jan 1 only when Jan 1 falls on a Monday; it begins on the previous Monday when Jan 1 falls on a Tuesday through Thursday; it begins on the subsequent Monday when Jan 1 falls on a Friday through Sunday.
J	The Julian day. Day one is equivalent to Jan 1, 4712 BC.
MI	The minute.
MM	The month number.
MON	The three-letter month abbreviation.
MONTH	The month name, fully spelled out.

Table 4. Date format elements (continued)

Format element	Function
Q	The quarter of the year. Quarter one is Jan–Mar, quarter two is Apr–Jun, and so forth.
RM	The month number in Roman numerals.
RR	The two-digit year.
RRRR	The four-digit year.
SCC	Same as CC, but negative for BC dates.
SP	A suffix that converts a number to its spelled format (e.g., ONE, FOUR). See TH.
SPTH	A suffix that converts a number to its spelled and ordinal form (e.g., FIRST, FOURTH). See TH.
SS	The second.
SSSSS	The number of seconds since midnight.
SYEAR	The year spelled out in words with a leading negative sign when the year is BC. See YEAR.
SYYYY	The four-digit year with a leading negative sign when the year is BC.
'text'	Quoted text to be reproduced in the output.
TH	A suffix, which can appear at the end of any format element, resulting in a number (e.g., *DD*th), and which results in the ordinal version of the number (e.g., 1st, 4th).
TS	Returns a time in a *short-time* format, which depends on NLS_TERRITORY and NLS_LANGUAGE. May be combined with only DL or DS.
TZD	The abbreviated time zone name (e.g., EST, PST, etc.).
TZH	The hour portion of the time zone displacement from UTC (Coordinated Universal Time) (e.g., -05 for U.S. EST).
TZM	The minute portion of the time zone displacement (usually zero).
TZR	The time zone region (e.g., "U.S./Eastern").
W	The week of the month. Week one starts on the first of the month; week two starts on the eighth of the month; and so forth.
WW	The week of the year.
X	The local radix character (e.g., the period [.] in American English).

Table 4. Date format elements (continued)

Format element	Function
Y	The last digit of the year number.
Y,YYY	The four-digit year with a comma after the first digit.
YEAR	The year spelled out in words.
YY	The last two digits of the year number.
YYY	The last three digits of the year number.
YYYY	The four-digit year.

When you use a date format element that displays a text value, such as the name of a month, the case used for the format element drives the case used in the output.

Table 5 shows examples of formatting dates.

Table 5. Date format examples

Format	Result
dd-mon-yyyy	13-dec-2002
dd-Mon-yyyy	13-Dec-2002
DD-MON-YYYY	13-DEC-2002
Month dd, yyyy	December 13, 2002
mm/dd/yyyy	12/13/2002
Day	Friday
DL	Thursday, September 2, 2004
DS	09/02/2004
DS TS	09/02/2004 08:10:38 PM

SQL*Plus Command Reference

This section contains an alphabetic listing of all the SQL*Plus commands, with brief descriptions.

Comment Delimiters (/*...*/)

```
/*
comment_text
comment_text
comment_text
*/
```

The /* and */ delimiters set off a comment in SQL*Plus. Comments entered this way may span multiple lines. If you use /*...*/ in a script file, the comments are displayed on the screen when the script is executed. For example:

```
/* SQL*Plus script written 7-Jan-2000
   by Jonathan Gennick. */
```

Double Hyphen (--)

```
-- comment_text
```

The double hyphen can place a single-line comment in a SQL*Plus script. For example:

```
--Written 7-Jan-2000 by Jonathan Gennick
```

At Sign (@)

```
@{url|file} [argument [argument...]]
```

The at sign (@) executes a SQL*Plus script file. For example:

```
@$ORACLE_HOME/rdbms/admin/utlxplan
@http://Gennick.com/message.sql 2
```

In Oracle9i Database Release 1, only the Windows version of SQL*Plus allows you to identify a script file by its URL. In Oracle9i Database Release 2 and higher, all versions of SQL*Plus support this functionality. URLs may be HTTP or FTP.

In iSQL*Plus, you must specify a URL with the @ command; you cannot specify a filename.

Double At Sign (@@)

@{url | file} [argument [argument...]]

The double at sign (@@) is used within a script file to execute another script file from the same directory as the first. For example:

```
@@generate_emp_report
@@generate_pay_history_report '101'
```

In *i*SQL*Plus, you must specify a URL with the @@ command; you cannot specify a filename.

Forward Slash (/)

/

A forward slash executes the SQL statement or PL/SQL block that is currently in the buffer. For example:

```
SQL> SELECT * FROM dual
  2
SQL> /

D
-
X
```

ACCEPT

```
ACC[EPT] variable [NUM[BER] | CHAR | DATE
                  |BINARY_FLOAT | BINARY_DOUBLE]
       [FOR[MAT] format_specification]
       [DEF[AULT] default_value]
       [PROMPT prompt_text | NOPR[OMPT]]
       [HIDE]
```

The ACCEPT command (not supported in *i*SQL*Plus) gets input from a user. For example:

```
ACCEPT user_password CHAR -
   PROMPT "Password: " HIDE
ACCEPT id NUMBER FORMAT "999.99"
ACCEPT report_date DATE -
   PROMPT "Date: " FORMAT "dd-mon-yyyy"
```

The *format_specification* may optionally be enclosed within quotes. CHAR is the default datatype. Use HIDE if you don't wish to echo the user's response.

APPEND

```
A[PPEND] text
```

APPEND (not supported in *i*SQL*Plus) is an editing command that lets you add text onto the end of the current line in the SQL buffer. For example:

```
SQL> L
  1* SELECT *
SQL> a FROM dual
  1* SELECT * FROM dual
```

The *text* is the text you want appended to the current line.

TIP

Use two spaces after the APPEND command if you want your appended string to begin with one space.

ARCHIVE LOG

```
ARCHIVE LOG {LIST |
             STOP |
             START [TO destination] |
             NEXT [TO destination] |
             ALL [TO destination] |
             log_sequence_number [TO destination]}
```

The ARCHIVE LOG command controls—or displays information about—archive logging. You must be connected as SYSDBA, SYSOPER, or INTERNAL to use this command. For example:

```
ARCHIVE LOG LIST
ARCHIVE LOG START
ARCHIVE LOG ALL TO /m01/oradata
```

The *destination* parameter specifies a destination, often a directory path, for archived log files.

ATTRIBUTE

```
ATTRIBUTE [object_type.attribute
          |attribute_alias [option [option...]]

option ::= {ALI[AS] alias |
            CLE[AR] |
            FOR[MAT] format_spec |
            LIKE source_attribute |
            ON |
            OFF}
```

The ATTRIBUTE command formats attributes of an Oracle object type. For example:

```
ATTRIBUTE employee_type.employee_salary -
    ALIAS emp_sal
ATTRIBUTE emp_sal FORMAT "$999,999.99"
ATTRIBUTE employee_type.employee_salary -
    FORMAT "$999,999.99"
```

Issuing the ATTRIBUTE command with no parameters displays a list of all current attribute settings.

The ALIAS, CLEAR, FORMAT, LIKE, ON, and OFF clauses function just as they do in the COLUMN command.

BREAK

```
BRE[AK] [ON element_action [ON element_action...]]

element_action ::= {element [action_1 [action_2]]
                    |element [action_2 [action_1]]}

element ::= {column_name | ROW | REPORT}

action_1 ::= SKI[P] {lines_to_skip | PAGE}

action_2 ::= {NODUP[LICATES] | DUP[LICATES]}
```

The BREAK command defines page breaks and line breaks based on changing column values in a report. It controls whether duplicate values print in a column and the printing of computed values such as totals and subtotals. Issuing the

break on report
compute sum of <col> on report

(sum for whole report)

BREAK command with no parameters causes SQL*Plus to display the current break setting. Following are some valid BREAK commands:

```
BREAK ON ROW SKIP 1
BREAK ON dept
BREAK ON dept SKIP PAGE
```

BTITLE

```
BTITLE [OFF | ON] | option [option...]

option ::= {COL x |
            S[KIP] x |
            TAB x |
            LE[FT] |
            CE[NTER] |
            R[IGHT] |
            BOLD |
            FOR[MAT] format_spec |
            text |
            variable}
```

BTITLE defines a page footer. For example:

```
BTITLE S 1 CE "Confidential! Do Not Copy"
```

When using BTITLE, you should start off with one of the keywords. Otherwise, if the first parameter after the command is just text, SQL*Plus will assume that you have used a now-obsolete syntax for this command, and you won't get the results you want.

For the variable parameter, you may use a substitution variable, or you may list one of the special variables maintained by SQL*Plus that are listed in Tables 1–6, under TTITLE.

CHANGE

```
C[HANGE] /old_text[/[new_text[/]]
```

CHANGE (not supported in *i*SQL*Plus) is an editing command that lets you do a search and replace on the current line in the SQL buffer. The CHANGE command can also delete text. For example:

```
SQL> l
  1* select dummy,smarty from duap
SQL> c /duap/dual/
  1* select dummy,smarty from dual
SQL> c /,smarty/
  1* select dummy from dual
```

A forward slash is commonly used to delimit the old and new text strings, but any other character may be used as long as it is not a number or letter—and as long as it is used consistently throughout the command.

CLEAR

```
CL[EAR] {BRE[AKS] | BUFF[ER] | COL[UMNS]
        |COMP[UTES] | SCR[EEN] | SQL TIMI[NG]}
```

The CLEAR command allows you to easily delete all column definitions, break settings, compute definitions, and so forth. For example:

```
CLEAR BREAKS
CLEAR COMPUTES
```

COLUMN

```
COL[UMN] [column_name [ALI[AS] alias |
                       CLE[AR] |
                       ENTMAP {ON | OFF} |
                       FOLD_A[FTER] |
                       FOLD_B[EFORE] |
                       FOR[MAT] format_spec |
                       HEA[DING] heading_text |
                       JUS[TIFY] {LEFT|CENTER
                                 |CENTRE|RIGHT} |
                       LIKE source_column_name |
                       NEWL[INE] |
                       NEW_V[ALUE] sub_variable |
                       NOPRI[NT] |
                       PRI[NT] |
                       NUL[L] null_text |
```

```
              OLD_V[ALUE] sub_variable |
              ON |
              OFF |
              TRU[NCATED] |
              WOR[D_WRAPPED] |
              WRA[PPED]...]]
```

The COLUMN command formats report output for columnar reports. Issuing the COLUMN command with no parameters gets you a list of all current column formats. Following are some example commands:

```
COLUMN employee_name HEADING "Name" -
    FORMAT A20 WORD_WRAPPED
COLUMN employee_hire_date -
    HEADING "Hire Date" -
    FORMAT A12 JUSTIFY RIGHT
```

COLUMN commands are cumulative. Two COLUMN commands specifying two different settings for the same field are equivalent to one command specifying both parameters.

COMPUTE

```
COMP[UTE] [functions OF column_names ON breaks]

functions ::= function [function...]

function ::= {AVG | COU[NT] | MAX[IMUM] | MIN[IMUM]|
              NUM[BER]|STD | SUM | VAR[IANCE]}
              [LABEL label_text]

column_names ::= column_name [column_name...]

breaks ::= break [break...]

break ::= group_column_name | ROW | REPORT}...]
```

The COMPUTE command defines summary calculations needed in a report. You can use COMPUTE in conjunction with BREAK to calculate and print column totals, averages, minimum and maximum values, and so forth. These calculations are performed by SQL*Plus as the report runs. COMPUTE is a complex command and, to get results, must be used in conjunction with the BREAK command. For example:

```
BREAK ON project_id
COMPUTE SUM LABEL "Totals" OF hours_logged -
    ON project_id

BREAK ON project_id ON employee_id
COMPUTE SUM OF hours_logged -
    ON project_id, employee_id
```

Issuing COMPUTE with no parameters causes SQL*Plus to list all currently defined computations.

CONNECT

```
CONN[ECT] [username[/password][@connect] | / | ]
          [AS {SYSOPER | SYSDBA}]
```

The CONNECT command changes your database connection, logs in as a different user, or connects to the database in an administrative mode. For example:

```
CONNECT SYSTEM/MANAGER@EMPDB
CONNECT /
CONNECT SYSTEM/MANAGER AS SYSDBA
```

COPY

```
COPY [FROM connection] [TO connection]
     {APPEND|CREATE | INSERT | REPLACE}
     destination_table [(column_list)]
     USING select_statement
```

The COPY command allows you to use SQL*Plus as a conduit for transferring data between two Oracle databases. For example:

```
copy from jeff/bigkid@empdb -
create emp_names (id, name) -
USING SELECT employee_id, employee_name -
    FROM employee
```

WARNING

COPY is not being enhanced to handle datatypes and features introduced with or after Oracle8i Database. COPY is a deprecated command, and may be removed in some future release of SQL*Plus.

DEFINE

```
DEF[INE] [variable_name [= text]]
```

The DEFINE command allows you to create a user variable (or substitution variable) and to assign it a value. Here's an example:

```
DEFINE company_name = "The Fictional Company"
```

You can also use DEFINE to list the value of one variable or to list the values of all variables, as shown in the following examples:

```
DEFINE company_name
DEFINE
```

DEL

```
DEL [{b | * | L}[ {e | * | L}]]
```

The DEL command (not supported in iSQL*Plus) is an editing command that deletes one or more lines from the buffer. For example:

```
DEL *
DEL 2 3
DEL 2 L
```

The b and e parameters are line numbers. Use L to refer to the last line of the buffer. Use an asterisk (*) to refer to the current line.

DESCRIBE

DESC[RIBE] [*schema.*]*object_name*[@*database_link_name*]

The DESCRIBE command displays information about a table, a view, an object type, a stored package, a stored procedure, a stored function, or a synonym. For example:

```
DESCRIBE employee
DESCRIBE jenny.employee
DESCRIBE employee@other_db
```

See also: SET DESCRIBE (under SET).

DISCONNECT

DISC[ONNECT]

The DISCONNECT command closes your database connection without terminating SQL*Plus.

EDIT

ED[IT] [*filename*]

The EDIT command (not supported in *i*SQL*Plus) allows you to invoke an external editor to edit the contents of the SQL buffer:

```
EDIT
```

Alternately, you can use EDIT to edit the contents of an operating system file:

```
EDIT $ORACLE_BASE/admin/orcl/pfile/init.ora
```

You can specify the command that invokes the external editor via the _EDITOR user variable. Use the DEFINE command to change _EDITOR's value.

EXECUTE

EXEC[UTE] *statement*

The EXECUTE command executes a single PL/SQL statement. For example:

```
EXECUTE DBMS_OUTPUT.PUT_LINE('Hi There');
```

EXIT

```
EXIT [SUCCESS | FAILURE | WARNING | value
     |sub_variable | :bind_variable]
     [COMMIT | ROLLBACK]
```

The EXIT command terminates a SQL*Plus session and returns to the operating system. For example:

```
EXIT
EXIT SUCCESS
EXIT FAILURE ROLLBACK
```

The default is to exit with a SUCCESS status, as well as to commit any outstanding transaction.

GET

```
GET filename [LIS[T] | NOL[IST]]
```

The GET command (not supported in iSQL*Plus) reads a SQL statement from a file and loads it into the buffer. For example:

```
GET my_report.sql
GET my_report NOLIST
```

Use LIST (the default) or NOLIST to control whether the contents of the file are displayed after being loaded.

HELP

```
HELP [topic]
```

The HELP command is used to get help on SQL*Plus commands. Prior to the release of Oracle8i Database, HELP also provided information on SQL and PL/SQL syntax. HELP is used as follows:

```
HELP INDEX
HELP DESCRIBE
```

The topic is the help topic you want to read about. Entering HELP INDEX (HELP MENU in some older releases) displays a complete list of valid topics.

TIP

Some Windows versions of SQL*Plus, notably those pri-
or to Oracle9i Database, do not support online help.

HOST

HO[ST] [os_command]

The HOST command (not supported in iSQL*Plus) allows
you to execute an operating system command or to invoke
the command interpreter so that you can execute several
such commands. Issuing HOST without specifying a command displays a command prompt from which you may
enter several commands. To return to SQL*Plus, you typi-
cally issue the operating system *exit* command.

INPUT

I[NPUT] [text]

The INPUT command (not supported in iSQL*Plus) inserts
one or more lines of text into the buffer, after the current
line. The *text* parameter is the text you want to insert. Use
this if you are inserting only one line. When you issue the
INSERT command with no text after it, SQL*Plus places you
into insert mode, allowing you to type as many lines as you
like. For example:

```
SQL> L
  1  SELECT
  2* FROM dual
SQL> L 1
  1* SELECT
SQL> I *
SQL> L
  1  SELECT
  2  *
  3* FROM dual
```

∧C

LIST

```
L[IST] [{b | * | L}[ {e | * | L}]]
```

The LIST command is an editing command that lists the current line from the buffer. Issuing LIST by itself displays all lines in the buffer. For example:

```
SQL> L
  1  SELECT
  2  *
  3* FROM dual
SQL> L 2 *
  2  *
  3* FROM dual
SQL> L 1 L
  1  SELECT
  2  *
  3* FROM dual
```

The *b* and *e* parameters are line numbers. Use L to refer to the last line of the buffer. Use an asterisk (*) to refer to the current line.

PASSWORD

```
PASSW[ORD] [username]
```

The PASSWORD command (not supported in *i*SQL*Plus) allows you to change your Oracle password using SQL*Plus. For example:

```
SQL> PASSWORD
Changing password for JONATHAN
Old password: ********
New password: ********
Retype new password: ********
Password changed
```

The *username* is the user whose password you want to change. The default is to change your own password. You need the ALTER USER privilege to change another user's password.

PAUSE

PAU[SE] [*pause_message*]

The PAUSE command (not supported in *i*SQL*Plus) tells SQL*Plus to display a message (optional) and pause. The user must then press the ENTER key to continue. For example:

PAUSE "Press ENTER to continue."

PRINT

PRI[NT] [*bind_variable_name*]

The PRINT command displays the value of a bind variable. For example:

PRINT x

If you omit a bind variable name, the values of all bind variables are printed.

PROMPT

PRO[MPT] *text_to_be_displayed*

The PROMPT command displays a message for the user to see.

TIP

The prompt string should not be quoted. If you include quotes, they will appear in the output.

QUIT

QUIT [SUCCESS | FAILURE | WARNING | *value*
    |*sub_variable* | :*bind_variable*]
    [COMMIT | ROLLBACK]

QUIT functions identically to EXIT.

RECOVER

The syntax of the RECOVER command (not supported in
*i*SQL*Plus) changes frequently. Because many changes were
introduced in Oracle Database 10*g*, this section contains separate syntax descriptions for Oracle9*i* Database and Oracle
Database 10*g*.

The RECOVER command initiates media recovery on a database, tablespace, or datafile. To use RECOVER, you must be
connected as SYSDBA or SYSOPER. Here are some examples:

```
RECOVER TABLESPACE USERS
RECOVER DATABASE UNTIL -
    TIME 20-JAN-2000:16:57:00
```

The hyphen (-) at the end of the first line in the second
RECOVER example is the SQL*Plus continuation character.
You must use continuation characters to continue a
RECOVER command across a line break.

WARNING

Do not use the RECOVER command unless you fully understand database recovery procedures.

Oracle9*i* Database Release 2 syntax

```
RECOVER {general | managed | END BACKUP}

general ::=
    [AUTOMATIC] [FROM directory]
    { {full_database_recovery
      |partial_database_recovery
      | LOGFILE filename}
      [recovery_option [recovery_option...] ]
    | CONTINUE [DEFAULT] | CANCEL}

full_database_recovery ::=
    [STANDBY] DATABASE
    [UNTIL {CANCEL | TIME datetime | CHANGE scn}]
    [USING BACKUP CONTROLFILE]
```

```
or
   [STANDBY] DATABASE
   [USING BACKUP CONTROLFILE]
   [UNTIL {CANCEL | TIME datetime | CHANGE scn}]

partial_database_recovery ::=
   {TABLESPACE tablespace_name [, tablespace_name]...
   | DATAFILE datafile_name [, datafile_name]...
     STANDBY {TABLESPACE tablespace_name
     [, tablespace_name]...
              | DATAFILE datafile_name
                        [, datafile_name]...}
   UNTIL [CONSISTENT] [WITH] CONTROLFILE }

recovery_option ::=
   {TEST | ALLOW blocks CORRUPTION
   | PARALLEL [degree] | NOPARALLEL}

managed ::=
   MANAGED STANDBY DATABASE
   [ {NODELAY | [TIMEOUT] minutes
   | CANCEL [IMMEDIATE] [NOWAIT]}
   | [DISCONNECT [FROM SESSION] ] [FINISH [NOWAIT] ] ]
```

AUTOMATIC

Automatically determines the names of the redo log files to apply during recovery.

FROM *directory*

Specifies the directory in which archived redo log files can be found.

LOGFILE *filename*

Begins recovery using the specified archived redo log file.

CONTINUE [DEFAULT]

Continues an interrupted multi-instance recovery. Use CONTINUE DEFAULT to have Oracle determine the next log file to apply.

CANCEL

Terminates cancel-based recovery.

STANDBY
> Recovers the standby database using control and archived redo log files from the primary database.

DATABASE
> Initiates media recovery on the entire database. The database must be mounted but not open.

UNTIL CANCEL
> Allows you to recover one log file at a time, with the opportunity to cancel after each log file has been processed.

UNTIL TIME *datetime*
> Performs a time-based recovery. All transactions completed prior to the time specified are recovered.

UNTIL CHANGE *scn*
> Performs an incomplete recovery based on the system change number (SCN). Note that the transaction with the specified number is not recovered.

USING BACKUP CONTROLFILE
> Causes recovery to use a backup control file.

TABLESPACE *tablespace_name*
> Initiates media recovery on the specified tablespace or list of tablespaces (up to a maximum of 16). The tablespace(s) must be offline, and the database must be mounted and open.

DATAFILE *datafile_name*
> Initiates media recovery on the specified datafile or list of datafiles. The datafiles to be recovered must be offline. As long as none of the datafiles are part of the SYSTEM tablespace, the database may remain open.

STANDBY TABLESPACE *tablespace_name*
> Recovers specified tablespace(s) in the standby database.

STANDBY DATAFILE *datafile_name*
> Recovers specified datafile(s) in the standby database.

UNTIL CONSISTENT WITH CONTROLFILE

Recovers the standby database using the standby database's control file.

TEST

Performs a trial recovery in which redo is read and applied in memory, but in which the database files themselves are left untouched.

ALLOW *blocks* CORRUPTION

Specifies the number of corrupt blocks to tolerate in the log files being applied during recovery. You can exceed one block only when also using the TEST option.

PARALLEL [*degree*]

Specifies that recovery be done in parallel, and optionally the degree of parallelism to use. The default degree of parallelism is the number of CPUs available on all instances multiplied by the value of the PARALLEL_THREADS_PER_CPU initialization parameter.

NOPARALLEL

Specifies that the recovery be done serially.

MANAGED STANDBY DATABASE

Places the standby database into sustained recovery mode.

NODELAY

Applies archived log files to the standby database without delay. Overrides any delay setting in LOG_ARCHIVE_DEST.

TIMEOUT *minutes*

Specifies a timeout, after which standby recovery will terminate if no log file is available to be applied.

CANCEL [IMMEDIATE] [NOWAIT]

Terminates standby recovery after applying the current archived redo log file. Use IMMEDIATE to terminate on the next log file read. NOWAIT functions like IMMEDI-ATE, except that the command returns control to you immediately.

DISCONNECT [FROM SESSION]

Creates a background process to apply redo to the standby database, so that you can do other work in your session.

FINISH [NOWAIT]

Use in the event that the primary fails to finish applying all primary log files to the standby. By default, the command waits for recovery to finish. Use NOWAIT to have control return to you immediately.

Oracle Database 10g syntax

```
RECOVER {general | managed | bracket}

general ::= [AUTOMATIC] [FROM location]
            {full_recovery | partial_recovery
             | LOGFILE filename}
            [general_option [general_option...]]

managed ::= MANAGED STANDBY DATABASE
             {managed_recovery | cancel | finish}

bracket ::= {BEGIN BACKUP | END BACKUP}

full_recovery ::= [STANDBY]DATABASE
                    [full_option [full_option...]]

partial_recovery ::= {partial_type
                       | STANDBY partial_type}
                      UNTIL [CONSISTENT WITH]
                      CONTROLFILE

general_option ::= {TEST
                     | ALLOW integer CORRUPTION
                     | parallel}

managed_recovery ::= managed_recovery_option
                      [managed_recovery_option...]
```

```
cancel ::= CANCEL [IMMEDIATE] [WAIT | NOWAIT]

finish ::= [DISCONNECT [FROM SESSION]] [parallel]
           FINISH [SKIP [STANDBY LOGFILE]]
           [WAIT | NOWAIT]

full_option ::= {UNTIL {CANCEL | TIME datetime
                       | CHANGE integer}
                       | USING BACKUP CONTROLFILE}

partial_type ::= {TABLESPACE tablespace_name
                  [, tablespace_name...]
                | DATAFILE {filename|filenumber}
                  [, filename | filenumber...]}

managed_recovery_option ::=
                    {{DISCONNECT [FROM SESSION]
                    | TIMEOUT integer | NOTIMEOUT}
                    | {NODELAY | DEFAULT DELAY
                    | DELAY integer}
                    | NEXT integer
                    | {EXPIRE integer | NO EXPIRE}
                    | parallel
                    | USING CURRENT LOGFILE
                    | UNTIL CHANGE integer
                    | THROUGH {[THREAD integer]
                              SEQUENCE integer
                              | ALL ARCHIVELOG
                    | {ALL | LAST | NEXT} SWITCHOVER}

parallel ::= {NOPARALLEL | PARALLEL [degree]}
```

AUTOMATIC

Automatically determines the names of the redo log files to apply. The default is to prompt you for each name.

FROM *location*

Specifies the directory in which archived redo log files are located. The default is to use the location specified by the LOG_ARCHIVE_DEST or LOG_ARCHIVE_DEST_1 initialization paremeters.

LOGFILE *filename*

Begins media recovery with the specified log file.

MANAGED STANDBY DATABASE
Places a standby database into sustained recovery mode, in which logs from the primary are automatically applied.

BEGIN BACKUP
Moves all database files into online backup mode.

END BACKUP
Moves all database files out of online backup mode.

STANDBY DATABASE
Initiates recovery of the standby database.

UNTIL [CONSISTENT WITH] CONTROLFILE
Recovers datafiles in standby database until they are consistent with the standby database's control file.

TEST
Initiates a trial recovery for the purpose of detecting problems that would occur during a real recovery. Redo is applied in memory, but none of the resulting data blocks are written to disk.

ALLOW *integer* CORRUPTION
Specifies the number of corrupt blocks to allow before aborting a recovery operation.

CANCEL [IMMEDIATE] [WAIT | NOWAIT]
Terminates recovery. Specify no options to terminate recovery after the current archived redo log file is applied. Use IMMEDIATE to cancel after the next redo log read, or after the current redo log file is applied, whichever comes first. Use WAIT to have the command wait for the termination. The default is to WAIT. Use NOWAIT if you wish to get back to the SQL*Plus command prompt without waiting for the termination to actually occur.

DISCONNECT [FROM SESSION]
Causes recovery to proceed in the background, freeing up your session for other work.

FINISH [SKIP [STANDBY LOGFILE]] [WAIT | NOWAIT]
Initiates recovery of any remaining, unapplied redo logs against the standby database. Use the SKIP clause to skip the application of standby redo log files. Use NOWAIT to get a command prompt back immediately, without waiting for the recovery operation to finish. Use WAIT to specify the default behavior, in which the command waits for the operation to finish.

UNTIL CANCEL
Performs recovery one log file at a time until you cancel the operation.

UNTIL TIME *datetime*
Recovers up through a date and time, which you should specify using the format 'YYYY-MM-DD:HH24:MI:SS'.

UNTIL CHANGE *integer*
Recovers up through a specified system change number (SCN).

USING BACKUP CONTROLFILE
Uses the backup control file as the basis for recovery.

TABLESPACE *tablespace_name*
Specifies a tablespace to be recovered.

DATAFILE *filename*
Specifies a datafile to be recovered.

filenumber
Specifies the number of a datafile to be recovered.

TIMEOUT *integer*
Specifies a timeout, in minutes, after which, if a requested archive redo log is not made available to the standby database, recovery terminates.

NOTIMEOUT
Explicitly requests the default behavior of sustained recovery with no timeout.

NODELAY
> Overrides any DELAY setting in LOG_ARCHIVE_ DEST_*n*.

DEFAULT DELAY
> Delays application of a redo log file by the number of minutes specified in LOG_ARCHIVE_DEST_*n*.

DELAY *integer*
> Overrides the DELAY setting in LOG_ARCHIVE_ DEST_*n* with a new timeout, specified in minutes.

NEXT *integer*
> Overrides any default DELAY and applies the next *integer* log files as soon as they can be applied.

EXPIRE *integer*
> Sets the number of minutes for which managed recovery will run, after which the operation will terminate.

NOEXPIRE
> Removes any expiration time that may have been set for a managed recovery operation.

USING CURRENT LOGFILE
> Recovers redo from standby online logs, obviating the need to archive them first.

THROUGH [THREAD *integer*] SEQUENCE *integer*
> Performs a managed standby recovery up through the specified thread and log sequence number.

THROUGH ALL ARCHIVELOG
> Performs a managed standby recovery until all logs have been applied.

THROUGH {ALL | LAST | NEXT} SWITCHOVER
> Continues a managed recovery through all switchover operations, only through the next switchover, or through the last switchover.

NOPARALLEL
Specifies that recovery be done serially.

PARALLEL [*degree*]
Specifies that recovery be done in parallel and, optionally, the degree of parallelism to use. The default degree of parallelism is the number of CPUs available on all instances multiplied by the value of the PARALLEL_THREADS_PER_CPU initialization parameter.

REMARK

```
REM[ARK] comment_text
```

The REMARK command is used to place comments in a SQL*Plus script. For example:

```
REM This script written by my dog.
```

REPFOOTER

```
REPF[OOTER] [PAGE] [OFF | ON] | option [option...]

option ::= {COL x |
            S[KIP] x |
            TAB x |
            LE[FT] |
            CE[NTER] |
            R[IGHT] |
            BOLD |
            FOR[MAT] format_spec |
            text |
            variable}
```

The REPFOOTER command defines a report footer. Report footers print on the last page of a report—after the last detail line and before the bottom title. See TTITLE or BTITLE for examples of the parameters being used.

REPHEADER

```
REPH[EADER] [PAGE] [OFF | ON] | option [option...]

option ::= {COL x |
             S[KIP] x |
             TAB x |
             LE[FT] |
             CE[NTER] |
             R[IGHT] |
             BOLD |
             FOR[MAT] format_spec |
             text |
             variable}
```

The REPHEADER command defines a report header. Report headers print on the first page of a report—after the page title and before the first detail line. See TTITLE or BTITLE for examples of the parameters being used.

RUN

```
R[UN]
```

The RUN command displays and then executes the command currently in the SQL buffer. For example:

```
SQL> R
  1* SELECT USER FROM dual

USER
------------------------------
JONATHAN
```

SAVE

```
SAV[E] filename [CRE[ATE] | REP[LACE] | APP[END]]
```

The SAVE command (not supported in *i*SQL*Plus) writes the contents of the SQL buffer to an operating-system file. For example:

```
SAVE my_query.sql
SAVE my_query REPLACE
```

The default file extension is .sql.

SET

> SET *parameter_setting*

The SET command customizes the SQL*Plus operations to your needs. For example:

```
SET DEFINE OFF
SET SERVEROUTPUT ON SIZE 1000000 -
    FORMAT WORD_WRAPPED
SET NULL '***'
```

Parameter settings

SET APPI[NFO] {OFF | <u>ON</u> | *app_text*}

Controls automatic registration of command files using the DBMS_APPLICATION_INFO package.

SET ARRAY[SIZE] {<u>15</u> | *array_size*}

Sets the number of rows SQL*Plus returns at one time from the database when executing a query.

SET AUTO[COMMIT] {ON | <u>OFF</u> | IMMEDIATE | *statement_count* }

Controls whether SQL*Plus automatically commits your changes. Also specifies the number of statements to allow between each commit.

SET AUTOP[RINT] {ON | <u>OFF</u>}

Controls whether SQL*Plus automatically prints the contents of bind variables after they have been referenced in a SQL statement or PL/SQL block.

SET AUTORECOVERY {ON | <u>OFF</u>}

When turned on, allows the RECOVER command to run without user intervention.

SET AUTOT[RACE] {ON | <u>OFF</u> | TRACE[ONLY]} [EXP[LAIN]] [STAT[ISTICS]]

Enables and disables the automatic display of the execution plan and execution statistics for a SQL statement.

set autotrace traceonly statistics

SET BLO[CKTERMINATOR] {. | *term_char* | ON | OFF}
Sets the character used to terminate entry of a PL/SQL block. The default is a period.

SET BUF[FER] {*buffer_name* | SQL}
Allows you to switch between buffers. Note that only the SQL buffer can be used for executing SQL statements.

SET CLOSECUR[SOR] {ON | OFF}
Controls whether SQL*Plus keeps the statement cursor open all the time.

SET CMDS[EP] {ON | OFF | *separator_char*}
Controls whether you can enter multiple SQL statements on one line and also sets the separator character. If you turn this option on, the default separator character is a semicolon.

SET COLSEP *column_separator*
Controls the text that separates columns of data. The default is to separate columns using one space. set colsep " "

SET COM[PATIBILITY] {V7 | V8 | NATIVE}
Specifies the Oracle release with which SQL*Plus should be compatible. The default behavior is to let SQL*Plus decide this automatically.

SET CON[CAT] {ON | OFF | *concat_char*}
Specifies the concatenation character that marks the end of a substitution variable name in a SQL*Plus command, SQL statement, or PL/SQL block. The default character is a period.

SET COPYC[OMMIT] *batch_count*
Controls how often SQL*Plus commits during the execution of a COPY command. The default is 0.

SET COPYTYPECHECK {ON | OFF}
Controls whether type checking is done when using the COPY command to copy data from one table to another.

SET DEF[INE] {<u>ON</u> | OFF | *prefix_char*}

Specifies the character that defines a substitution variable. The default is the ampersand character (&).

SET DESCRIBE [DEPTH {1 | *levels* | ALL}] [LINENUM {ON | <u>OFF</u>} [INDENT {<u>ON</u> | OFF}

Specifies behavior for the DESCRIBE command. DEPTH controls the level to which to recursively describe an object (e.g., a table might contain an object column, which in turn might contain a nested table, etc.). LINENUM adds line numbers to DESCRIBE's output. INDENT causes descriptions of nested objects to be indented.

SET DOC[UMENT] {<u>ON</u> | OFF}

Controls whether SQL*Plus displays documentation demarcated by the DOCUMENT command.

SET ECHO {ON | <u>OFF</u>}

Controls whether SQL*Plus displays commands from a command file as they are executed.

SET EDITF[ILE] *edit_filename*

(not supported in *i*SQL*Plus)

Specifies the name of the work file used when you invoke an external editor using the EDIT command. The default name is *afiedt.buf*.

SET EMB[EDDED] {ON | <u>OFF</u>}

Enables and disables the embedded report feature. This allows you to combine two reports into one without resetting the page numbering.

SET ESC[APE] {ON | <u>OFF</u> | *escape_char*}

Specifies the escape character, which is used in front of the substitution variable prefix character (usually an ampersand, or &), when you want that character interpreted literally and not as part of a variable name. The default character is a backslash (\).

SET FEED[BACK] {ON | OFF | 6 | *row_threshold*}
    Controls whether and when SQL*Plus displays the number of rows affected by a SQL statement. *and PL/SQL succ.compl message*

SET FLAGGER {OFF | ENTRY | INTERMED[IATE] | FULL}
    Controls whether SQL*Plus checks your statements for compliance with ANSI/ISO syntax.

SET FLU[SH] {ON | OFF}
    (not supported in *i*SQL*Plus)
    Controls whether output may be buffered.

SET HEA[DING] [ON | OFF]
    Controls whether column headings are displayed when selecting data.

SET HEADS[EP] {ON | OFF | *heading_separator*}
    Controls the character used to make a line break in a column heading. The default is a vertical bar (|).

SET INSTANCE [*service_name* | LOCAL]
    Specifies the default net service name to use with the CONNECT command.

SET LIN[ESIZE] *line_width*
    Specifies the size of a line in terms of characters. The default LINESIZE is 80 characters.

SET LOBOF[FSET] *offset*
    Specifies an index into a LONG column, indicating the first character to be displayed. The default is 1.

SET LOGSOURCE *logpath*
    Tells SQL*Plus where to find archive log files for recovery. There is no default.

SET LONG *long_length*
    Specifies the maximum number of characters to display from a column of type LONG. The default is 80.

SET LONGC[HUNKSIZE] *size*

>Controls the number of characters retrieved from a LONG column at one time. The default is 80.

SET MAXD[ATA] *max_row_width*

>Sets the maximum row length that SQL*Plus can handle. This is an obsolete setting, and there is no default.

SET MARKUP ::= HTML [ON | OFF] [HEAD "*text*"] [BODY "*text*"] [TABLE "*text*"] [ENTMAP {ON | OFF}] [SPOOL {ON | OFF} [PREFORMAT {ON | OFF}]

>Allows you to specify the markup language to use when generating output. You must specify the HTML option; the other options are optional.

>HTML [ON | OFF]

>>Specifies whether or not to use HTML as the markup language.

>HEAD "*text*"

>>Specifies content for the <head> tag. The tag ends up being written as <head>*text*</head>.

>BODY "*text*"

>>Specifies content for the <body> tag. The tag ends up being written as <body *text*>.

>TABLE "*text*"

>>Specifies content for the <table> tag used to format query output. The tag ends up being written as <table *text*>.

>ENTMAP {ON | OFF}

>>Controls whether SQL*Plus uses HTML equivalents such as < and > for special characters such as "<" and ">".

>SPOOL {ON | OFF}

>>Controls whether SQL*Plus writes <head> and <body> tags to the spool file when spooling HTML output.

PRE[FORMAT] {ON | <u>OFF</u>}
> Controls whether spooled report output is enclosed within \<pre>...\</pre> tags instead of being placed in an HTML table.

SET NEWP[AGE] {*lines_to_print* | NONE}
> Controls the number of lines SQL*Plus prints between pages. A value of zero causes SQL*Plus to print a form feed character between each page. The default is 1.

SET NULL *null_text*
> Controls the text SQL*Plus uses to represent a null value. The default is to represent nulls by a space.

SET NUMF[ORMAT] *format_spec*
> Sets the default display format for numbers. There is no default value.

SET NUM[WIDTH] {<u>10</u> | *width*}
> Sets the default display width for numbers. SET NUMFORMAT takes precedence over this value.

SET PAGES[IZE] *lines_on_page*
> Specifies the number of printable lines on a page. The default is 24. *If 0, will remove headings*

SET PAU[SE] {ON | <u>OFF</u> | *pause_message*}
> Controls whether SQL*Plus pauses after each page of output.

SET RECSEP {<u>WR[APPED]</u> | EA[CH] | OFF}
> Controls whether a record-separator line is printed between lines of output. The default is to print separators only when one of the column values in a record has wrapped.

SET RECSEPCHAR *separator_char*
> Controls the character used for the record separator. The default record separator is a line of space characters.

SET SCAN {<u>ON</u> | OFF}

Enables and disables user variable substitution. This option is obsolete in favor of SET DEFINE.

SET SERVEROUT[PUT] {ON | <u>OFF</u>}
[SIZE *buffer_size*] [FOR[MAT] {WRA[PPED] |
WOR[D_WRAPPED] | TRU[NCATED]}

Controls whether SQL*Plus prints output from PL/SQL blocks.

SET SHIFT[INOUT] {VIS[IBLE] | <u>INV[ISIBLE]</u>}
(not supported in *i*SQL*Plus)

Controls the display of shift characters on IBM 3270 terminals.

SET SHOW[MODE] {ON | <u>OFF</u> | BOTH}
(not supported in *i*SQL*Plus)

Controls whether SQL*Plus displays the before and after values when you change a setting.

SET SPACE *num_of_spaces*

Specifies the number of spaces to print between columns. The default is 1. This option is obsolete in favor of SET COLSEP.

SET SQLBLANKLINES {ON | <u>OFF</u>}
(not supported in *i*SQL*Plus)

Controls whether you may enter blank lines as part of a SQL statement. Introduced in Release 8.1.5.

SET SQLC[ASE] {<u>MIXED</u> | UPPER | LOWER}

Controls automatic case conversion of SQL statements and PL/SQL blocks.

SET SQLCO[NTINUE] *continuation_prompt*
(not supported in *i*SQL*Plus)

Allows you to change the continuation prompt used for multiline SQL statements. The default is the greater-than symbol (>).

SET SQLN[UMBER] {<u>ON</u> | OFF}
(not supported in *i*SQL*Plus)

Controls whether SQL*Plus uses the line number as a prompt when you enter a multiline SQL statement.

SET SQLPLUSCOMPAT[IBILITY] *version.release*[*.update*]

Specifies that SQL*Plus will act in a manner compatible with a prior release of the software. For example, SET SQLPLUSCOMPATIBILITY 10.1.0.

SET SQLPRE[FIX] *prefix_char*
(not supported in *i*SQL*Plus)

Specifies the SQL*Plus prefix character that allows you to execute a SQL*Plus command while entering a SQL statement or PL/SQL block into the buffer. The default is a pound sign (#).

SET SQLP[ROMPT] *prompt_text*
(not supported in *i*SQL*Plus)

Allows you to change the SQL*Plus command prompt. The default is SQL>.

SET SQLT[ERMINATOR] {<u>ON</u> | OFF | *term_char*}

Controls whether terminating a SQL statement using the semicolon causes it to be executed. Also allows you to change the termination character to something other than a semicolon.

SET SUF[FIX] *extension*
(not supported in *i*SQL*Plus)

Specifies the default extension used for command files. The default is *.sql*.

SET TAB {<u>ON</u> | OFF}
(not supported in *i*SQL*Plus)

Controls whether SQL*Plus uses tab characters to format whitespace.

SET TERM[OUT] {<u>ON</u> | OFF}
(not supported in *i*SQL*Plus)

Controls whether SQL*Plus displays output generated from a SQL*Plus script file.

SET TI[ME] {ON | <u>OFF</u>}
(not supported in *i*SQL*Plus)

Controls whether SQL*Plus displays the current time as part of the command prompt.

SET TIMI[NG] {ON | <u>OFF</u>}

Controls whether SQL*Plus displays the elapsed execution time for each SQL statement or PL/SQL block.

SET TRIM[OUT] {<u>ON</u> | OFF}
(not supported in *i*SQL*Plus)

Controls whether SQL*Plus trims trailing spaces from lines displayed on the screen.

SET TRIMS[POOL] {ON | <u>OFF</u>}
(not supported in *i*SQL*Plus)

Controls whether SQL*Plus trims trailing spaces from lines written to a spool file.

SET TRU[NCATE] {ON | <u>OFF</u>}

Controls whether SQL*Plus truncates long lines.

SET UND[ERLINE] {*underline_char* | {<u>ON</u> | OFF}}

Sets the character used to underline column headings. The default is a hyphen.

SET VER[IFY] {<u>ON</u> | OFF}

Controls whether SQL*Plus displays before and after images of lines containing substitution variables.

SET WRA[P] {<u>ON</u> | OFF}

Controls whether SQL*Plus wraps or truncates long lines.

SHOW

```
SHO[W] { setting
    ALL |
    BTI[TLE] |
    ERR[ORS]
        [{FUNCTION | PROCEDURE | PACKAGE | PACKAGE BODY
        | TRIGGER | TYPE | TYPE BODY | VIEW}
        [owner.]object_name] |
    LNO |
    PARAMETER[S] [parameter_name] |
    PNO |
    REL[EASE] |
    REPF[OOTER] |
    REPH[EADER] |
    SGA |
    SPOO[L] |
    SQLCODE |
    TTI[TLE] |
    USER}
```

The SHOW command allows you to look at the current state of your SQL*Plus environment. For example:

```
SHOW PARAMETER db_block_buffers
SHOW LINESIZE
SHOW TTITLE
```

You may also use SHOW ERRORS to see error messages resulting from an attempt to create a stored procedure, function, or other such object.

SHUTDOWN

```
SHUTDOWN [NORMAL | IMMEDIATE
        | TRANSACTIONAL [LOCAL] | ABORT]
```

The SHUTDOWN command allows you to stop an Oracle instance. In order to use SHUTDOWN, you must be connected as SYSDBA or SYSOPER. For example:

```
SHUTDOWN
SHUTDOWN IMMEDIATE
```

Use NORMAL to wait for users to voluntarily disconnect, IMMEDIATE to disconnect each user as soon as his current statements complete, TRANSACTONAL to disconnect users as their transactions complete, TRANSACTIONAL LOCAL if you do not care to wait for distributed transactions to complete, and ABORT to terminate the instance immediately. If you use ABORT, then you have essentially crashed the instance, and crash recovery will take place when you next open the instance.

SPOOL

```
SP[OOL] file_name [option] | OFF | OUT

option ::= {CRE[ATE] | REP[LACE] | APP[END]}
```

The SPOOL command (not supported in *i*SQL*Plus) causes output to be written to a text file. For example:

```
SPOOL c:\data\emp_pay_report
SPOOL OFF
```

The default extension depends on the operating system and is usually either *.lst* or *.lis*. A path may be specified as part of the filename.

START

```
STA[RT] {script_file | url} [argument [argument...]]
```

START executes a SQL*Plus script. See "At Sign (@)" for an example. START and @ function identically.

STARTUP

```
STARTUP {options | upgrade_options}

options ::= [FORCE] [RESTRICT]
            [PFILE=parameter_filename]
            [QUIET] [mount]

mount ::= {MOUNT [database_name]
          | OPEN [open_options]
          | NOMOUNT}
```

```
open_options ::= {READ {ONLY | WRITE [RECOVER]}
                  | RECOVER}

upgrade_options ::= [PFILE=parameter_filename]
                    {UPGRADE | DOWNGRADE}
                    [QUIET]
```

The STARTUP command allows you to start an Oracle instance and open a database. For example:

```
STARTUP
STARTUP RESTRICT
STARTUP PFILE = c:\temp\tempinit.ora
```

To use STARTUP, you must be connected as SYSDBA or SYSOPER.

When you use the PFILE option, SQL*Plus reads the parameter file, not the Oracle instance, and thus the path to the parameter file must be relative to the machine running SQL*Plus.

STORE

```
STORE SET filename [CRE[ATE] | REP[LACE] | APP[END]]
```

The STORE command (not supported in iSQL*Plus) generates a file of SET commands based on the current state of those settings. For example:

```
STORE SET current_settings REPLACE
...
@current_settings
```

In this example, the first command stores the current settings; the second command restores those settings by executing the file generated by the STORE command.

TIMING

```
TIMI[NG] [START timer_name] | SHOW | STOP]
```

The TIMING command lets you start, stop, or display the value of a timer in order to measure elapsed time. Here's an example:

```
TIMING START emp_query_timer
TIMING SHOW
TIMING STOP
```

TTITLE

```
TTITLE [OFF | ON] | option [option...]

option ::= {[COL x |
             S[KIP] x |
             TAB x |
             LE[FT] |
             CE[NTER] |
             R[IGHT] |
             BOLD |
             FOR[MAT] format_spec |
             text |
             variable]}
```

The TTITLE command defines page titles for a report. For example:

```
TTITLE CENTER 'The Fictional Company' SKIP 3 -
LEFT 'I.S. Department' -
RIGHT 'Project Hours and Dollars Report'

TITLE RIGHT FORMAT 999 SQL.PNO
```

Issuing the TTITLE command with no parameters causes SQL*Plus to display the current setting.

For the variable parameter, you may specify a substitution variable, or you may list one of the system variables maintained by SQL*Plus. These are described in Table 6.

Table 6. SQL*Plus system variables

System variable	Value
SQL.PNO	The current page number
SQL.LNO	The current line number
SQL.RELEASE	The current Oracle release
SQL.SQLCODE	The error code returned by the most recent SQL query
SQL.USER	The Oracle username of the user running the report

UNDEFINE

    UNDEF[INE] variable_name [variable_name...]

The UNDEFINE command erases a user variable definition. For example:

    UNDEFINE emp_name
    UNDEFINE emp_name proj_name

The *variable_name* is the name of a user variable to delete. You can delete several variables with one command by listing them separated by spaces.

VARIABLE

    VAR[IABLE] var_name data_type

The VARIABLE command declares bind variables. For example:

    VARIABLE x NUMBER
    VARIABLE query_results REFCURSOR
    VARIABLE emp_name VARCHAR2(40)

Bind variables are real variables that can be used within a PL/SQL block or SQL statement. Issuing the VARIABLE command with no parameters generates a list of all currently defined bind variables.

Handwritten annotations:

or, break on manager-id
column manager-id new-value mgr-var noprint
TTITLE left 'Manager: ' mgr-var skip 2
select ...
where manager-id in ('101', '102')
order by manager-id;

SQL*Plus supports the following datatypes for use with bind variables:

NUMBER
> Results in a floating-point number and is the same as a NUMBER variable in PL/SQL or a NUMBER column in a table. Unlike PL/SQL, SQL*Plus does not let you specify a length or a precision, so a declaration like NUMBER (9,2) is not allowed.

BINARY_FLOAT
> Results in a BINARY_FLOAT value. Not available before Oracle9i Database.

BINARY_DOUBLE
> Results in a BINARY_DOUBLE value. Not available before Oracle9i Database.

CHAR [(length [CHAR | BYTE])]
> Results in a fixed-length character string. The length is optional. If it is omitted, you get a one-byte string.

NCHAR [(length)]
> Results in a fixed-length character string in the national character set. The length is optional. If it is omitted, you get a one-character string.

VARCHAR2 (length [CHAR | BYTE])
> Results in a variable-length character string.

NVARCHAR2 (length)
> Results in a variable-length character string using the national language character set.

CLOB
> Results in a character large object (CLOB) variable.

NCLOB
> Results in a CLOB variable using the national language character set.

REFCURSOR

Gives you a cursor variable you can use to return the results of a SQL query from PL/SQL to SQL*Plus.

WHENEVER

```
WHENEVER {OSERROR | SQLERROR}
        {EXIT [SUCCESS | FAILURE | value
             | :bind_variable | sub_variable]
            [COMMIT | ROLLBACK]
        | CONTINUE [COMMIT | ROLLBACK | NONE]}
```

The WHENEVER command controls the behavior of SQL*Plus when an operating system error or a SQL error occurs. For example:

```
WHENEVER OSERROR EXIT FAILURE
WHENEVER SQLERROR EXIT FAILURE ROLLBACK
WHENEVER SQLERROR CONTINUE
```

WHENEVER SQLERROR EXIT SQL.SQLCODE;

Index

Symbols

() (parentheses), controlling join
    order, 30
(+) (plus sign in parentheses),
    specifying outer joins, 28
. (period)
    terminating SQL statements
        with, 8
-- (double hyphen), single-line
    comment, 97
/ (forward slash), 98
/*...*/ (comment delimiters), 97
@ (single at sign), executing
    script files, 98
@@ (double at sign), executing
    script files, 98

A

ACCEPT command, 98
    formatting data, 93
access method hints, 85
    FULL, 85
    INDEX, 85
    INDEX_JOIN, 86
    NO_INDEX, 86
adduser command, 15

admin user, 15
aggregate functions, 38
aliases for column names, 21
ALL keyword, 40, 54
ALL_ROWS hint, 85
APPEND command, 10, 54, 99
APPEND hint, 89
ARCHIVE LOG command, 100
as_of-clause, 43
ASC keyword, 20
at sign (@), 98
at sign, double (@@), 98
ATTRIBUTE command, 100
AVG function, 38

B

Beaulieu, Alan, 1
bind variables, 10
blank lines in SQL statements, 8
BLOCKTERMINATOR
    command, 9
BREAK command, 68, 100
browser-based version of
    SQL*Plus (see iSQL*Plus)
BTITLE command, 67
buffers, SQL, 8

We'd like to hear your suggestions for improving our indexes. Send email to
index@oreilly.com.

O

ON clause, 30, 33
  USING clause and, 59
optimizer goal hints, 85
  ALL_ROWS, 85
  CHOOSE, 85
  FIRST_ROWS, 85
  RULE, 85
optimizer hints, 83–89
optional tables, specifying, 28
Oracle Database 10g
  connecting to iSQL*Plus, 11
  DBMS_XPLAN, 80
  deleting rows after update, 61
  flashback queries, 43
  formatting time, 94
  hint query blocks, 84
  iSQL*Plus, 13
  join order hints, 86
  merging data, 59
  MODEL clause, 44–52
  obsolete optimizer goal
    hints, 85
  partition outer joins, 35
  plan table, 78
  query transformation
    hints, 88
  RECOVER command, 115
  using aggregate functions, 38
*Oracle Database Performance
  Tuning Guide*, 82
*Oracle SQL*Plus: The Definitive
  Guide*, 1
Oracle9i
  CASE expressions, 25
  COALESCE function, 24
  connecting to iSQL*Plus, 12
  DBMS_XPLAN, 80
  default port number for
    iSQL*Plus, 11
  flashback queries, 43
  full outer joins, 32

identifying script file by
  URL, 97
inserting data, 52
invoking SQL*Plus, 4
join conditions, specifying, 33
merging data, 59
multitable inserts, 54
online help and, 108
optimizer goal hints, 85
RECOVER command, 111
table joins, 28
VARIABLE command, 136
ORDER BY clause, 42
  GROUP BY clause and, 39
  table joins and, 30, 37
ORDERED hint, 86
ORDERED_PREDICATES
  hint, 89
outer joins, 31
  in Oracle8i, 28
output, plain text, 16

P

page breaks, controlling, 68
page headers/footers,
  defining, 67
page headings, 75
page length/width,
  controlling, 66
PAGESIZE setting, 66, 72
parentheses (), controlling join
  order, 30
PARTITION BY clause, 36
partition outer joins, 35–37
partitions, specifying, 42
PASSWORD command, 109
PAUSE command, 110
period (.)
  terminating SQL statements
    with, 8
plain text output, 16

Related Titles Available from O'Reilly

Oracle PL/SQL

Learning Oracle PL/SQL

Oracle PL/SQL Best Practices

Oracle PL/SQL Developer's
Workbook

Oracle PL/SQL Language
Pocket Reference,
3rd Edition

Oracle PL/SQL Programming,
3nd Edition

Oracle Books for DBAs

Oracle DBA Checklists
Pocket Reference

Oracle RMAN
Pocket Reference

Unix for Oracle DBAs
Pocket Reference

Oracle SQL and SQL Plus

Mastering Oracle SQL

Oracle SQL Plus:
The Definitive Guide

Oracle SQL Tuning
Pocket Reference

Oracle SQL*Plus
Pocket Reference, *2nd Edition*

Oracle SQL:
The Essential Reference

Oracle

Building Oracle XML
Applications

Java Programming with
Oracle JDBC

Oracle Application Server 10g
Essentials

Oracle Essentials:
Oracle Database 10g,
3nd Edition

Oracle in a Nutshell

Perl for Oracle DBAs

TOAD Pocket Reference

O'REILLY®

Keep in touch with O'Reilly

1. Download examples from our books

To find example files for a book, go to:
www.oreilly.com/catalog

select the book, and follow the "Examples" link.

2. Register your O'Reilly books

Register your book at *register.oreilly.com*

Why register your books? Once you've registered your O'Reilly books you can:

- Win O'Reilly books, T-shirts or discount coupons in our monthly drawing.
- Get special offers available only to registered O'Reilly customers.
- Get catalogs announcing new books (US and UK only).
- Get email notification of new editions of the O'Reilly books you own.

3. Join our email lists

Sign up to get topic-specific email announcements of new books and conferences, special offers, and O'Reilly Network technology newsletters at:
elists.oreilly.com

It's easy to customize your free elists subscription so you'll get exactly the O'Reilly news you want.

4. Get the latest news, tips, and tools
www.oreilly.com

- "Top 100 Sites on the Web"—PC Magazine
- CIO Magazine's Web Business 50 Awards

Our web site contains a library of comprehensive product information (including book excerpts and tables of contents), downloadable software, background articles, interviews with technology leaders, links to relevant sites, book cover art, and more.

5. Work for O'Reilly

Check out our web site for current employment opportunities:
jobs.oreilly.com

6. Contact us

O'Reilly & Associates
1005 Gravenstein Hwy North
Sebastopol, CA 95472 USA

TEL: 707-827-7000 or 800-998-9938
(6am to 5pm PST)

FAX: 707-829-0104

order@oreilly.com
> For answers to problems regarding your order or our products.
> To place a book order online, visit:
> *www.oreilly.com/order_new*

catalog@oreilly.com
> To request a copy of our latest catalog.

booktech@oreilly.com
> For book content technical questions or corrections.

corporate@oreilly.com
> For educational, library, government, and corporate sales.

proposals@oreilly.com
> To submit new book proposals to our editors and product managers.

international@oreilly.com
> For information about our international distributors or translation queries. For a list of our distributors outside of North America check out:
> *international.oreilly.com/distributors.html*

adoption@oreilly.com
> For information about academic use of O'Reilly books, visit:
> *academic.oreilly.com*

O'REILLY®

Our books are available at most retail and online bookstores.
To order direct: 1-800-998-9938 • *order@oreilly.com* • *www.oreilly.com*
Online editions of most O'Reilly titles are available at *safari.oreilly.com*